EXPLORING GWENT

45 SELECTED WALKS
IN
THE BLACK MOUNTAINS, THREE PEAKS OF ABERGAVENNY, VALE OF USK, WENTWOOD, COASTAL PLAIN, WESTERN VALLEYS, COBBLER'S PLAIN, WYE VALLEY AND THE LAND OF THE TRILATERAL CASTLES

D0474642

Front cover picture:
On top of the world at Pen-fford-goch Pond (popularly known as Keeper's Pond) on Blorenge Mountain, with the Sugar Loaf in the distance (see Route 6)

OTHER TITLES BY THE SAME AUTHOR

WALKS IN THE BRECON BEACONS (Out of print)
EXPLORING THE WATERFALL COUNTRY (Out of print)
GHOSTS OF WALES
EXPLORING THE BRECON BEACONS NATIONAL PARK
MYSTERIOUS WALES

EXPLORING GWENT

A Walker's Guide to Gwent — Land of History and Legend

Monnow Bridge, Monmouth
18th century engraving

Chris Barber

Regional Publications (Bristol) Limited

First published in Great Britain 1984
by Regional Publications (Bristol) Limited,
3 & 5 St Paul's Road, Clifton,
Bristol, BS8 1LX
and
5 Springfield Road,
Abergavenny,
Gwent, NP7 5TD

All photographs by the Author
except where indicated

Copyright © 1984
Chris Barber

ISBN 0 906570 13 1

This book is copyright under the
Berne Convention. All rights are
reserved. Apart from any fair dealing
for the purpose of private study,
research, criticism or review, as
permitted under the Copyright Act 1956,
no part of this publication may be
reproduced, stored in a retrieval
system, or transmitted in any form,
or by any means, electronic,
electrical, chemical, mechanical,
optical, photocopying, recording or
otherwise, without the prior
permission of the copyright owner.
Enquiries should be addressed to
the publishers.

Printed by South Western Printers Ltd.,
Caerphilly, Mid-Glamorgan, South Wales

TO MY PARENTS WHO FIRST TAUGHT
ME HOW TO WALK AND IN MEMORY
OF FRED HANDO THE WALKING
HISTORIAN OF GWENT

PLEASE REMEMBER, WHEN WALKING IN GWENT:

Take nothing but photographs
Kill nothing but time, and
Leave nothing but your footprints
and goodwill

Contents

The Vale of Usk, 72

Wentwood Area, 89

The Coastal Plain, 95

Cobbler's Plain and Trellech Ridge, 110

Wye Valley, 119

General Information, 141

Introduction

This guide describes forty-five walking routes that explore some of my favourite corners of Gwent. Many of the walks have historical associations and they are mainly circular routes. However, several fairly lengthy linear routes have been included, and these are best undertaken by joining up with a friend and positioning a car at each end of the walk. Unfortunately it is not always possible to time your walk to fit in with rural public transport, particularly if you are walking on a Sunday.

For convenience, I have divided the county into easily identified areas. Gwent is a county of remarkable scenic variety; said by some to possess the most varied scenery for its size of any county in England and Wales. It is certainly an excellent county for the walker to explore, with some two-and-a-half thousand miles of footpaths. In addition, it is well endowed with prehistoric sites, Roman remains, Norman castles, ancient churches, historic houses, mountains, river valleys, woodlands and superb vantage points.

The countryside is constantly changing, particularly in farming areas; hedges may be removed, footpaths ploughed or barbed wire introduced. A grass field may be a cornfield on your next visit, stiles turned into gates and vice versa. Even barns may be demolished — just to confuse the intrepid map reader. However, I hope that the changes that you encounter on your travels are not too drastic!

Every effort has been made to provide accurate route descriptions of all the walks, but no doubt walkers will find a few changes or problems. I would be grateful for news of any route finding difficulties or other problems so that subsequent editions of the book may be brought up to date.

Many years of intensive exploration and historical research have gone into the production of this book and I am now pleased to be able to share the pleasures of my wanderings with all who make use of my guide to the walks of Gwent.

I would like to thank everyone who has helped me in the production of this book. In particular, Ann Waller my editor and publisher and my than   are also due to Roger Millet for drawing the maps. I am also grateful to the many other friends who gave me their encouragement.

Barber
Gwent 1984

Llanfoist, Ab

9

In Appreciation
of Fred J. Hando
(1888—1970)

I count myself very fortunate to have known Fred Hando, a popular local historian who was devoted to Gwent and spent most of his life researching, sketching and writing about the antiquities, legends and history of this county.

In my youth I often accompanied my father, Bill Barber (author of *West of the Wye*) and Fred Hando on journeys into Gwent, exploring hidden corners of the countryside, and felt the magic of his enthusiasm which undoubtedly inspired me to follow in his footsteps as a writer about Gwent.

During his long association with the *South Wales Argus*, Fred Hando wrote the amazing total of 795 articles about Gwent and many of these were subsequently published in seven books.

Several memorial seats have been erected at vantage points in the county at locations which this historian used to visit on his wanderings. The seats were erected from the proceeds of a special fund launched by the Monmouthshire Local History Council and the *South Wales Argus*.

Guidelines for Walkers

"Over hill, over dale,
Through bush and through brier,
Over park, over dale,
Through flood and through fire,
I do wander everywhere."

Puck's Song from *A Midsummer Night's Dream*

William Shakespeare

The majority of the walks in this book are country rambles and the routes given in the hill areas are fairly safe and easy to follow. No doubt the following reminders will be unnecessary for the majority of readers, but they are offered as a guide to walkers of limited experience.

1. Plan walks with a generous time allowance.
2. In winter take warm and windproof clothes. Even in summer carry a spare sweater when walking on high ground.
3. Always carry an Ordnance Survey 1:50,000 or 1:25,000 map (a compass can often prove useful as well and should always be carried on hill walks).
4. Carry spare food, torch, whistle and first aid kit.
5. Wear sensible footwear. Be prepared to meet mud and stinging nettles! Boots are advisable for the hill walks and either boots or wellingtons can make muddy farm tracks less daunting.
6. Always carry waterproofs.
7. Carry your spare clothing and equipment in a small lightweight rucksack.
8. If you plan to lead a large party around one of the routes (e.g. a rambling club) it is always a good idea to check your route beforehand and if possible speak to landowners mentioning that you intend to lead a group of people on the rights of way across their land, and give the date. Even though you have every right to do this, it is wise to foster good relations and to ensure that you know your route and do not inadvertently trespass with a large party.

PUBLIC RIGHTS OF WAY

"To roam paths suddenly seen
Through leafy veils of radiant green"

Dafyd ap Gwilym
(14th century Welsh poet)

Our footpaths are a fascinating part of our history. Many of them are older than the Roman era and even date back to prehistoric times. The Romans were especially active in Gwent and left behind many reminders of their 300 year stay

11

in Britain. Their great forts were linked by straight tracks, many of which have now become surfaced highways, but others have disappeared completely.

A public right of way is either a footpath or a bridleway over which the public has a legal right of access. On footpaths one has the right of passage on foot only. Horses and bicycles may be ridden on bridleways but not motorised vehicles. These routes are all part of the highway system and subject to the same protection in law as a trunk road.

Roads used as public paths are known as RUPP's. These are usually green lanes or unsurfaced tracks which have never been used by enough traffic to deserve maintenance. Legally they are still open to all traffic but are generally unsuitable for vehicles. In the next few years they are likely to be re-classified as byways, bridleways or footpaths in accordance with the Countryside Act 1968.

Generally in Gwent, footpaths and bridleways are signposted at points where they leave a metalled road. The signposts indicate that the route is a public one and often show where it leads and the distance involved in kilometres.

To help those confused —

1 kilometre = 1,093 yards = 5/8th mile (nearly!) or 0.6214 miles (to be exact)

MAP READING

This guide should be used in conjunction with Ordnance Survey maps and it is not intended that the walker should rely just on the sketch maps. These are only included to provide a rough idea of the location of starting points and the direction of the route of the walk.

The Ordnance Survey 1:50,000 (approximately 1¼ inches to the mile) maps covering Gwent are Sheets 161, 162 and 171. On these maps public rights of way are shown as red dots for footpaths and red dashes for bridleways.

The Ordnance Survey 1:25,000 (2½ inches to the mile) maps (Second Series) available for Gwent at the present time are ST 29/39, ST 28/38, ST 48/58, SO 21/31 and SO 40/50. On these maps rights of way are shown as green dots for footpaths and green dashes for bridleways. These maps are easier to follow than the 1:50,000 because they show field boundaries — but a word of warning! Remember that the ground does not always match the map, as field boundaries are often found to be removed when farmers enlarge their fields.

Always make good use of landmarks to help you ascertain the route of a footpath when you are following it on the map, e.g. barns, roads, churches, woods and streams etc.

OBSTRUCTIONS

If you encounter an obstruction you are entitled to take the best way round it that you can find, or remove enough of it to make progress.

Climb any locked gates on the hinge end so as not to place too much leverage on the hinge.

BULLS IN FIELDS

It is an offence for the farmer to put a bull in a field crossed by a public right of way, except where the bull does not exceed ten months, or is not a recognised dairy breed and is accompanied by cows or heifers.

PLOUGHED PATHS

Sometimes it is impossible to see the route of a path because of ploughing. Where a path has been legally ploughed over, the occupier is now required to make good the surface so that it can be used as a right of way as soon as possible after ploughing and not later than two weeks from the time ploughing of the path began, unless weather conditions are exceptional.

CLOSURE AND DIVERSION OF PATHS

Landowners do not have the right to close or divert public rights of way. Such action can only be carried out through the correct procedures undertaken by the County Council.

WAYMARKING

In Gwent all waymarking of public paths follows the pattern recommended by the Countryside Commission. Yellow arrows are used for footpaths and blue arrows for bridleways. There is a total of 2,800 miles of footpath and bridleway in Gwent, so waymarking has only been carried out n a priority basis and largely applies to circular waymarked walks, problem spots on popular paths and linear routes such as the *Wye Valley Walk* or the *Usk Valley Walk*, which both carry a yellow dot in addition to the arrow to show that the route is a special one.

Sometimes the waymarks are vandalised and they may also fade and deteriorate owing to weather erosion, particularly in exposed locations. Walkers should always carry an Ordnance Survey map and not put too much reliance on waymarking to find their way.

★　★　★

"No man goes further than he who knows
not where he is going."

Oliver Cromwell

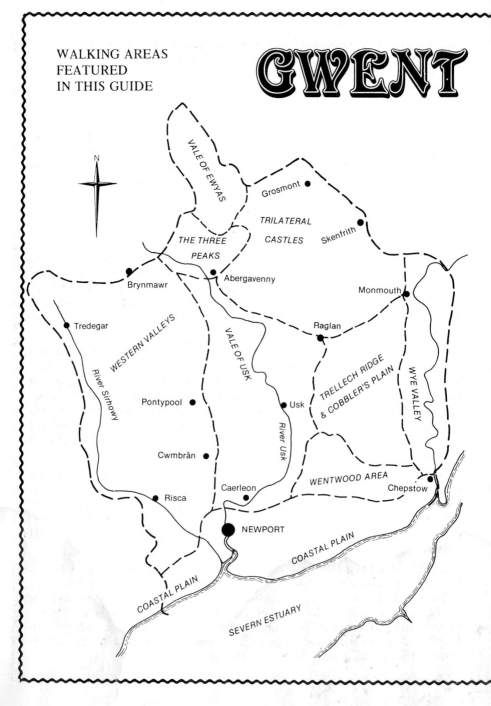

WALKING AREAS
FEATURED
IN THIS GUIDE

GWENT

N

VALE OF EWYAS

Grosmont

TRILATERAL CASTLES

Skenfrith

THE THREE PEAKS

Brynmawr

Abergavenny

Monmouth

Tredegar

WESTERN VALLEYS

Raglan

VALE OF USK

River Sirhowy

Pontypool

TRELLECH RIDGE & COBBLER'S PLAIN

WYE VALLEY

Usk

River Usk

Cwmbrân

Caerleon

WENTWOOD AREA

Chepstow

Risca

NEWPORT

COASTAL PLAIN

COASTAL PLAIN

SEVERN ESTUARY

Situated midway between the Equator and the North Pole, lying between 51°29' and 51°59' north latitude, is a small part of Wales known as Gwent. It is interesting to note that to the west at the same latitude are parts of Labrador and Newfoundland and, to the east, part of Siberia. In these locations they have extremely severe winters, yet in Gwent we are generally blessed with very mild weather, January 1982 being a rare exception!

This ancient Kingdom of Gwent derived its name from a Celtic word meaning *fair* and the area was known as "the fair land" from its natural beauty.

It was formed of three regions — Lower Gwent or Gwent Iscoed (Gwent below the wood), Upper Gwent or Gwent Uchoed (Gwent above the wood) and the boundary between these two areas was a large expanse of forest stretching from the river Usk at Caerleon to the river Wye. The third region was Blaina Gwent — a mountainous area to the north-west.

When the Romans arrived, they changed the name from Gwent to Siluria, because the area was occupied by a tribe known as the Silures. No other tribe in Britain proved so difficult to subdue. The Silures held out for nine years against the invading legions of Rome. Even after being subdued, the Romans found it necessary to station their crack legion (their version of the S.A.S.) — the Second Augustan — within this territory, at Caerleon, and here it remained during the full period of the Roman occupation of nearly 400 years.

When the Romans left Britain, the name Gwent came back into use and was generally used until the formation of the County of Monmouth under King Henry VIII. Monmouthshire came into being in 1536 when the Act of Union was passed abolishing the power of the Norman Lords Marcher, and their lands were divided to form seven new shires. The twenty-four lordships lying between the Rhymney and the Wye valleys were united to form Monmouthshire. This Act of 1536 conferred upon the newly formed County the right to send three members to represent the people in Parliament.

On the right bank of the Wye, the parish of Welsh Bicknor, which had once belonged to the Marcher Lordship of Monmouth, was an isolated fragment of Monmouthshire between neighbouring Gloucestershire and Herefordshire from 1536 to 1845. And, in the Black Mountains, a strip of hillside east of the Grwyne Fawr valley belonged to Herefordshire until 1893 when it was taken over by Monmouthshire.

In 1974, that unforgettable event known as Local Government re-organisation took place and on April 1st Monmouthshire once more became Gwent.

The shape of the County is that of an irregular parallelogram with a projection on the north comprising the valley of the Honddu. Gwent measures roughly 22 miles from east to west and 27 miles from north to south. It can surely be said that few areas in Britain contain so much variety of landscape, history and culture within such a small area.

In Praise of Gwent

"The God who made this county was an artist... the fellow who turned out Dorking was a Bank Holiday Tradesman by comparison."

George Bernard Shaw

"This county is not surpassed, if it be equalled, by any other part of this Kingdom. The delightful diversities of hills and dales, woods and water, cornfields and meadows, are so beautifully scattered throughout the county, that nature, wherever we turn our view, gives to art a rule of perfection for the ornamental and intrinsic improvement of almost every estate."

John Fox (1794)

"Enchanting views of pleasant landscapes, magnificent mountain ranges, interesting ruins of castles and monasteries, a great variety of manor houses and some splendid churches."

C.J.O. Evans (1953)

"Gwent has a greater variety in the style and size of its many churches than any other county in Wales. Every period is represented from Norman to Victorian, although the greater number are Perpendicular."

Maxwell Fraser

(There are approximately 230 churches in Gwent!)

"The older I grow the more firmly I am convinced that anything which I may have accomplished in literature is due to the fact that when my eyes were first opened in earliest childhood they had before them the vision of an enchanted land."

Arthur Machen
writing about Gwent

"Monmouthshire, which derives its name from the capital town... may be justly considered the connecting link between England and Wales; as it unites the scenery, manners and language of both."

Archdeacon William Coxe (1801)

Many historians have written about Gwent for it is a county rich with antiquity and history. The marks left by the Silurians, the Saxons, Normans can be seen throughout the county in many forms. historians to write in depth about this area was Archdeacon Coxe on horseback, made a thorough exploration and published his book entitled *Coxe's Tours in Monmouthshire* in 180 . This book proved to be the inspiration for many later writers and today it seems incredible that Coxe managed to unearth so many antiquities and cover so much of the county without the aid of detailed maps or modern transport.

The Vale of Ewyas

*"In this deep Vale of Ewyas about an arrow shot broad
and encircled on all sides by lofty mountains is a situation
truly calculated for religion and more adapted to canonical
discipline than all the monasteries of the British Isles."*

Giraldus Cambrensis (1188)

Vale of Ewyas above Llanthony

...and, to many, the most beautiful of the Black Mountains
...been praised by many pets and writers and the Priory of Llanthony
...ted by such great artists as J.M.W. Turner.

*"The Valley of Ewias lies, in 'nersed so deep and round,
As they below that see the ountains rise so hie,
Might think the straggling ferds were grazing in he skie."*

Michael Drayton (1613)

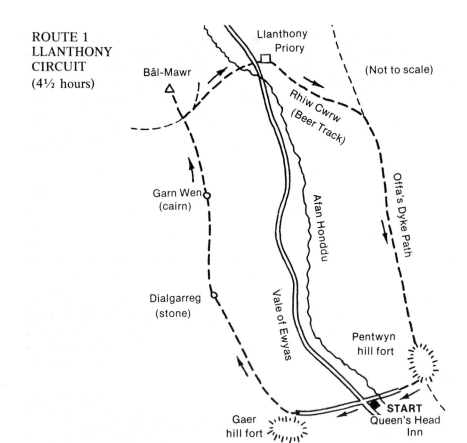

ROUTE 1
LLANTHONY
CIRCUIT
(4½ hours)

Bâl-Mawr

Llanthony
Priory

(Not to scale)

Rhiw Cwrw
(Beer Track)

Garn Wen
(cairn)

Afan Honddu

Offa's Dyke Path

Dialgarreg
(stone)

Vale of Ewyas

Pentwyn
hill fort

START
Queen's Head
Inn

Gaer
hill fort

*"Here the monks sitting in their Cloisters, enjoying the
fresh air, when they happen to look up towards the
horizon, behold the tops of the mountains as it were
touching the heavens and herds of wild deer feeding on
their summits."*

Giraldus Cambrensis (1188)

This route starts from the Queen's Head Inn (G.R. 312221) which is situated a
couple of miles up the Llanthony Valley (sometimes referred to as the Vale of
Ewyas) on the B4423.

Just north of the inn, turn immediately left to ascend a road leading up towards
the Gaer hill fort. After a long ascent the road becomes a cart track, which
reaches a gate and the open hillside. Here, one may detour to inspect the
earthworks of the hill fort or keep straight on along the main track. On the right
are views down into the Llanthony Valley and across to the crumbling cliffs of Old
Red Sandstone known locally as the Darren. On the left are views into the
Grwyne Fawr Valley.

18

In due course one encounters a small stone about 3 feet high set into the ground beside the track. Marked on the O.S. map as Dialgarreg, it is also known as "the stone of revenge", and marks the spot where Richard de Clare, a Norman lord, was ambushed and killed by the Welsh, led by Morgan ap Owen.

Continue along the ridge with magnificent views into the valleys on either side. Ahead will soon be seen the giant cairn of Garn-Wen. This is a tall circular cairn which has obviously been built with tender care and considerable skill. After about a mile another cairn is reached, below the hump of Bâl-Mawr. Turn right and descend towards Llanthony.

Take a track to the right leading down into Cwm-bwchel to follow a stony shelf down the side of the valley. Soon, ahead, Llanthony Priory can be seen and this is a good path from which to admire the magnificent setting of this fine ruin.

A stile is reached; then follow waymarks down to another stile, past a farmhouse to a metal gate. Straight on down to a wooden gate and then through a dingle beside a stream. Follow its right bank to reach a wooden gate/stile; then over another stile, directly opposite, into a field. Go down to a stile and then across a metal footbridge over the Afon Honddu and follow a track into the hamlet. Walk up the road to reach Llanthony Priory.

The name, Llanthony, is a corruption from Llan-Honddu (the church on the Honddu) or, more fully, Llan-Dewi-Nant-Honddu (the church of St David on the river Honddu), the first church there, according to tradition, having been erected by St David in the 6th century. It is reputed that during some period of his life he came to the Vale of Ewyas and erected a small chapel or cell on the banks of the Honddu.

Llanthony Priory *19th century engraving*

The Priory was founded in about 1107 by William de Lacy who was a brother of the Lord of Ewyas. Roger, Bishop of Salisbury, was responsible for much of the design and the west front is said to resemble portions of Salisbury Cathedral. The south tower and prior's house are now an hotel and the old gatehouse is now used as a barn by the adjoining farm.

In 1136 the Augustinian monks, having found the Welsh locals too unfriendly and the weather even worse, retreated (remarking that they "had no mind to sing to the wolves") to Gloucester to found a new priory which they also called Llanthony. Only a handful of monks were left in the Vale of Ewyas and Llanthony gradually became a place of banishment where offending brothers were sent to serve penance.

The poet, Walter Savage Landor, bought the estate in 1808 and had grand ideas of restoring the Priory to its former glory, but he quarrelled with his tenants and neighbours who obviously did not share his dreams. In 1813 he left the valley for good having squandered £70,000 on the estate. He wrote: "I shall never cease to wish that Julius Caesar had utterly exterminated the whole race of Britons. I am convinced that they are as irreclaimable as gypsies or Malays." He died in Florence in his 90th year in 1864.

Situated in a wood above the Priory are the remains of Landor's house which was never completed. It is known as "The Sharple" and the ruins are said to be haunted (presumably by Mr Landor).

After examining the ruins of the Priory and perhaps enjoying a cool drink in the vaulted bar of the hotel, go over a stile near Abbey Farm (off drive) and walk round the back of the Priory to reach another stile and a waymarked path signposted to Longtown. Follow this path beside a beautiful stone wall (built by volunteers and local craftsmen) to reach a stile. Then go diagonally up a field to a stile near the top right hand corner. Continue up through the woods to a stile and straight through the next field to another stile. Turn right (ignore yellow waymark to left, which is part of a waymarked walk) to follow the ancient track known as the Rhiw Cwrw (beer track), which was once used by monks travelling between Llanthony and Longtown, on the other side of the hill. The track may be very muddy in places, caused by pony trekking. It gently ascends the hillside with fine views across to the Sugar Loaf.

On reaching the crest of the ridge, turn right to follow Offa's Dyke Long Distance path. Views to the west show Graig Syffyrdin, Malvern and Clee Hills. One may often meet other walkers on this ridge slogging their way along the 168 mile journey from Sedbury to Prestatyn.

Pass a trig'point on the left and go down to the ramparts of Pentwyn hill fort. Follow a broad cart track to a metal gate and descend a tarmac road. At a corner by a cottage, take a track to the right leading down through the trees. On reaching a road, turn right and then left at the next junction to head back to the starting point.

ROUTE 2
CWMYOY CHURCH — *The most crooked building in Gwent.* (2 hours)

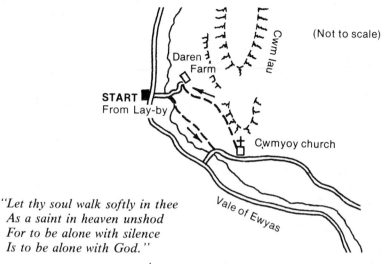

(Not to scale)

*"Let thy soul walk softly in thee
As a saint in heaven unshod
For to be alone with silence
Is to be alone with God."*

Anon

Follow the Llanthony Valley past the Queen's Head Inn and after nearly 3 miles, leave your car in a small layby beside a barn on the right hand side of the road, just before a road leading to the Cwmyoy Pony Trekking Centre (signposted Cwmyoy 1.6 km and G.R. 289243).

Cross the bridge over the river and go past a cottage to reach a stile. Then continue beside a wire fence and by the river to shortly ascend the bank on left. Turn right, following the hedge to a stile. Continue beside the hedge to a metal gate/stile. Cross three fields and stiles to reach a track leading to a road. Turn left and follow road up to Cwmyoy hamlet.

Situated on a hillside, the Church of St Martin appears to be toppling over and relies on several buttresses for support. Not only is the chancel out of line with the nave, but the walls and windows fall away to the south and the tower leans towards the mountain. It has been said that no part of the church is square or at right angles with any other part. These distortions have been caused by subsidence due to the instability of the underlying rock.

Of particular interest is the mediaeval cross inside the church which at one stage of its life found its way to an antique shop in London, but was subsequently recognised and recovered. There are also many old and very interesting tombstones in the churchyard which are worth perusing.

Cwmyoy should correctly be spelt *CWMIOU* — which means *"Valley of the Yoke"*, which refers to the cleft above the church, cutting into the hillside and caused by a landslip. The church hangs on in this position but the Old Black Lion Inn, which would have been a welcome sight to thirsty walkers, has long since gone.

Cwmyoy Church, Vale of Ewyas

After exploring the church, go up to a metal gate on the north side of the churchyard and then left along a metalled path. Shortly turn right up a stony track (signposted Graig 0.1 km) which ascends pleasantly between high banks to a metal gate.

Turn left, following the path past a wooden chalet and along a wide path (with good views) to reach a stream and a wooden gate. Then carry straight on, following a broad path. Above, can be seen the crumbling Old Red Sandstone cliffs of Darren, sometimes festooned with huge icicles in the winter.

Bear left at the path junction, by some stone walls and then descend, with good views across the valley, to reach a stile. Cross the field to another stile and then follow a fence down to the left and above a cottage to reach another stile.

Turn left and quickly right to a metal gate and left down the farm drive to reach the starting point.

★　★　★　★　★

The following route is situated in the Grwyne Fawr Valley to the west of the Vale of Ewyas and provides a reason for visiting Chwarel-y-Fan, which is the highest point in Gwent It also gives the walker additional views of the Llanthony Valley (Vale of Ewyas).

ROUTE 3
CHWAREL-Y-FAN (3 hours)

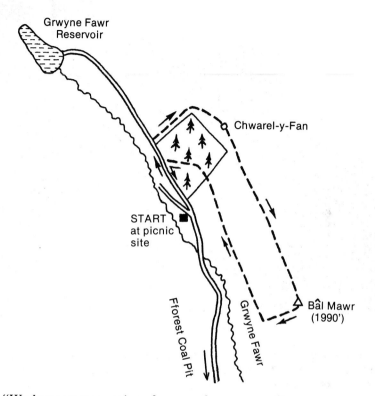

*"We love our mountains; because they are very fine
if a little undersized as mountains go..."*

Emlyn Williams

This is a pleasant hill walk in the upper reaches of the Grwyne Fawr Valley and takes you to the highest point in Gwent.

Just beyond Blaen-y-Cwm farm is a small picnic site on the banks of the Grwyne Fawr stream (G.R. 251286). Park here and follow the track on the east side of the valley which leads up to the Grwyne Fawr reservoir. This was at one time an old railway track, built to enable materials to be transported up the valley for the construction of the dam, which stands at an altitude of 1790 feet above sea level. When it was built in 1912, this was the highest reservoir in England and Wales and supplied water to Abertillery.

On reaching a gate across the track, go through and turn immediately right to follow a fence beside a Forestry Commission plantation. On reaching the end of the plantation go straight up to the crest of the ridge. Just over the crest of the ridge, turn right along a well defined path and head towards the cairn of

Chwarel-y-Fan, Black Mountains

Chwarel-y-Fan. Below now, to the left, is the Vale of Ewyas. This narrow ridge provides a fine viewpoint. Ahead is the Sugar Loaf and to the west can be seen the highest peaks of the Black Mountains, Waun Fach and Pen-y-Gader Fawr.

Continue along the narrow ridge over Bwlch-bach and Bwlch Isaf to reach the trig'point of Bâl-Mawr (1990 feet). Descend to the right (west of trig point), down a narrow but well defined path to reach a broad track contouring the hillside just above the tree line.

Turn right and follow this track for about two miles to reach a stile, directly ahead, giving access to a path leading through a plantation. Shortly, you will reach a forest road. Turn left and descend towards the Grwyne Fawr Valley. When the road turns in the opposite direction (i.e. southwards) shortly turn right, down a bridle path leading through the trees to reach a kissing gate. Turn left and follow earlier route to reach starting point.

Baldwin, Archbishop of Canterbury, and Giraldus, Archdeacon of Brecon, travelled through this valley on their return from preaching the Third Crusade in Wales. Their journey was described by the historian, Sir Richard Colt Hoare, in the following words:

> *"...they crossed the Black Mountains to the source of the Gronwy-Fawr river, which rises in that eminence and pursues its rapid course into the Vale of Usk. From thence a rugged and uneven tract descends suddenly into a narrow glen, formed by the torrent of the Gronwy, between steep impending Mountains, bleak and barren for the first 4 or 5 miles, but afterwards wooded to the very margin of the stream. A high ledge of grassy hills on the left hand, of which the principal is called the Bal, divides this formidable pass from the Vale of Ewyas, in which stands the noble monastery of Llanthoni, encircled by its mountains."*

24

The Three Peaks
of
Abergavenny

"Cloud shadows on the Sugar Loaf, the song a river sings
When touched by rain's soft finger tips, those sudden mellow gleams
Of sunlight on old Skirrid — these are the magic things
That I have stored within my heart and woven into dreams."

Myfanwy Haycock

There are three hills grouped around Abergavenny, often referred to as *"The Three Peaks"*. A popular endurance walk is organised by the Youth Hostels Association every year which traverses these hills and is eighteen miles in length. The hills are known locally as the Sugar Loaf, Skirrid Fawr and Blorenge.

ROUTE 4
MYNYDD PEN-Y-FAL
(*Sugar Loaf*)
(3 hours)

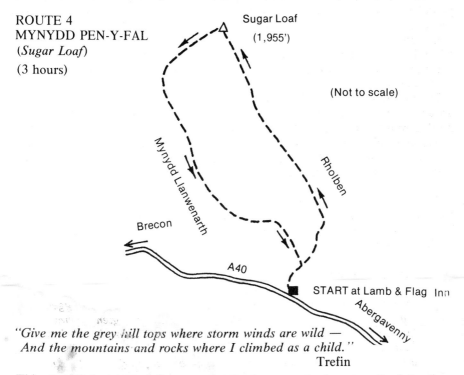

"Give me the grey hill tops where storm winds are wild —
And the mountains and rocks where I climbed as a child."
Trefin

This route is just one of the many interesting ways to the summit of the Sugar Loaf. Its Welsh name is *Mynydd Pen-y-fal* and at 1,955 feet it just fails to reach the magic height of 2,000 feet, yet it always seems to be a much higher mountain, for the approaches are quite long and the views from the summit very extensive.

Mynydd Pen-y-Fal (Sugar Loaf) from the summit of Skirrid Fawr

Start at the Lamb and Flag Inn which is conveniently situated just outside Abergavenny on the A40 (Brecon road G.R. 282153). From the car park, walk to the left of the inn to reach a stile. Keep the fence on your right to reach another stile at the end of the field. Turn right on to the road and then straight on at the junction. Go through a metal kissing gate on the left.

Cross the field to the top right hand corner and over a stile. Follow the hedge on right to a stile and almost immediately go over another stile. Up slightly to the right to reach a stile in the hedge. Then make for a metal gate in the top right hand corner of the field by Home Farm. Follow the hedge on your right to reach a stile opposite a cottage. Turn left on to the road and, after approximately 300 yards, turn right following an ascending road. Good views over Abergavenny and across to the Blorenge.

On reaching a National Trust sign (Sugar Loaf), follow a waymarked path branching left and giving direct access to the Rholben spur. Ascend a well defined path to the crest of the ridge. This is the traditional path up the Sugar Loaf from Abergavenny, with remnants of a metal seat positioned at a good vantage point, where the weary can rest their bones and contemplate the Usk Valley.

Soon the summit and ridge of Skirrid Fawr come into view on the right and shortly, ahead, can be seen the cone of the Sugar Loaf rising like an extinct volcano, which it is not. It was actually believed to be one in the early 19th century.

> *"It looks like a piked ridge from the opposite side of the Usk; sometimes appears in a globular shape, but at a distance and particularly at the south eastern side of Skyrrid, assumes the form of a pyramid and resembles the crater of a volcano. This cone is the highest object in the vicinity, has nothing rugged or craggy, and is characterised by smoothness and beauty."*
>
> Archdeacon William Coxe (1801)

The gradient eases and one no longer puffs and blows and can enjoy the view with more pleasure. After some distance, a junction of tracks is reached, where a broad track contours around the hillside. (A young boy in a school party I was once leading up the Sugar Loaf asked me with a gleam of enthusiasm in his eye, "Is that one of those contour lines that you mentioned, sir?").

Keep straight on to follow a path leading to the steeper summit slope. Scramble over the summit rocks and walk along the plateau to reach the trig' point.

The summit is about three hundred yards long and there is a cluster of rocks at the western end. On a clear day the extensive view ranges from the large mass of the Black Mountains to the north, the Usk Valley beyond Crickhowell with the Brecon Beacons in the far distance; Skirrid Fawr, eastern Gwent and across to the Malvern and Cotswold Hills. Abergavenny is spread out below and the river Usk can be seen winding its way towards the Severn Estuary. To the south is the bulky mass of the Blorenge, and on its right the limestone gorge of Clydach.

Just below the trig' point (south side), follow a track leading diagonally down

Ysgyrydd Fawr and Abergavenny   *(Route 5 overleaf)*   *19th century engraving*

27

and taking you to the top of the Mynydd Llanwenarth spur. Then down a deeply rutted path, straight on at the cross tracks and then branch left at the next junction. Follow a wide path down the spur and, on reaching some hollows in the ground, bear left towards a wood. On reaching a fence, follow it to the right to reach a road. Continue, past Pentre Farm and steeply down hill. At the bottom of the hill, go over a stile to right of a bridge. Follow the hedge on the left down to a stile giving access to the Lamb and Flag Inn.

ROUTE 5
SKIRRID FAWR (*Ysgyrydd Fawr*)
— THE HOLY MOUNTAIN (1,595 feet)
(2½ hours)

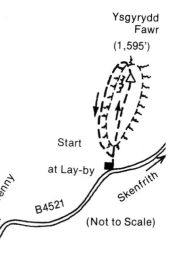

*"On fair clear days we could
see the pointed summit of
the Holy Mountain by Abergavenny.
It would shine I remember,
a pure blue in the far sunshine;
it was a mountain peak
in a fairy tale."*

Arthur Machen
"Far off things"

This isolated hill is situated to the north east of Abergavenny. Throughout the ages this peak has held the respect of men — locals and travellers alike. Undoubtedly this awe must be attributed to its unusual shape which has resulted in many tales and legends being woven around it.

Start at a layby on the B4521 approximately three miles northeast of Abergavenny (G.R. 329164). Near this parking area, on the Abergavenny side, is a stile signposted "Skirrid Fawr". Follow a path between two fences to the corner of a field to reach a stile giving access to a path ascending through the Skirrid wood to follow a series of steps. At the end of the Forestry Commission plantation, cross a stile and then turn right to pass through a picturesque dingle, to follow a waymarked path to the open hillside.

On joining the ridge, the view opens up on both sides. This ridge is approximately one mile in length with an easy gradient after the initial ascent. The trig' point is seen at the far end. On the west side are st cliffs where a massive landslip left a deep cutting. There are severai egends ch attempt to provide an explanation for this striking feature on the Skirrid. It has been suggested that it was caused by Noah's Ark passing over the mountain; or the heel mark left by a giant when he jumped here from the Sugar Loaf; or alternatively it was said to be caused by an earthquake at the time of the Crucifixion of Christ, when the "rocks were rent".

28

Archdeacon Coxe, during his historic tour of the County in 1801, wrote a dramatic description of his ascent of Skirrid Fawr.

> *"The heat was intense and the fatigue that I had undergone during the day was so considerable that when I looked down from the narrow and desolate ridge, the boundless expanse around and beneath, which suddenly burst upon my sight overcame me. I felt a mixed sensation of animation, lassitude, horror and delight. My spirits almost failed, even curiosity was suspended and I threw myself extended on the ground."*

Several times he tried to get up and walk along the ridge, but his head became so giddy when he looked down the "precipitous" slopes and particularly towards the great fissue that he could not remain on his feet.

> *"I seemed only safe when extended on the ground and was therefore in no condition to examine and describe the beauties of the view."*

The Archdeacon did of course manage to descend the Skirrid and continue with his travels and writings.

Near the summit is a hollow in the ground which was once the site of a Roman Catholic chapel dedicated to St Michael. Two upright stones were possibly part of the entrance. The panoramic views from this summit are very impressive.

If the walker is not happy about steep descents, he should return by the outward route, otherwise descend the steep northern slope. At the foot of the

The Blorenge Mountain from Abergavenny   (Route 6 overleaf)

slope, follow a track leading into the landslide valley. Notice a strange toadstoolshaped rock, known as The Devil's Table, on the hillside above. The path leads pleasantly down through the valley and then ascends slightly through the woods at the southern end of the hill. Rejoin the original path and return to the starting point.

ROUTE 6
THE BLORENGE (*Blawreng — Blueridge*) PLATEAU (2½ hours)

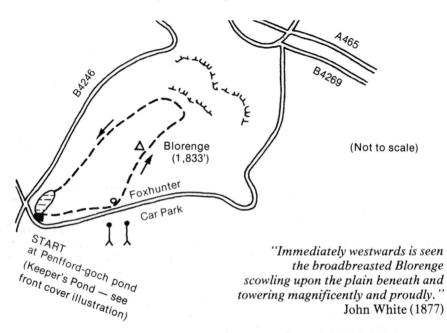

(Not to scale)

"Immediately westwards is seen the broadbreasted Blorenge scowling upon the plain beneath and towering magnificently and proudly."
John White (1877)

To the south west of Abergavenny stands the symmetrical hulk of the Blorenge. Sometimes it is referred to as the "Blancmange" and, indeed, when seen from the town, it has the appearance of being tipped straight out of a giant mould.

The energetic will climb this hill (1,833 feet) directly from Llanfoist, ascending the steep north east face. However, the following route provides the easiest way of reaching the summit and takes in the best viewpoints that are available from the summit plateau.

Start from Pen-fford-goch pond (Keeper's Pond) on the side of the B4246. This large pool was constructed as a header pond for supplying smaller ponds at Garnddyrys forge, an eighteenth century iron works on the slopes of the valley below (see Route 13). The pond was constructed in about 1820 and its name means *"Head of the red road"*. Early O.S. maps refer to it as Forge Pond.

From the pond follow a track (opposite the Pwll Du road) across the open hillside and towards two tall radio masts. On reaching a road, by the masts, turn left and walk to the Foxhunter car park. From here, follow a path leading to Foxhunter's grave, where a plaque bears the following inscription in memory of a great horse:

3rd April 1940 — 21st November 1959.
Here lies Foxhunter.
Champion International Show Jumper.

Winner of 78 International Competitions, including many foreign Grand Prix and the King George V Gold Cup 1948, 1950 and 1953.

35 times member of the British Show Jumping team which won Olympic Gold Medal at Helsinki 1952.

Bronze medals at London 1948, Prince of Wales Cup, London, five times (1949-1953) and the Aga Khan Cup outright, Dublin (1950, 1951-1953).

Just beyond this memorial is an iron boundary marker (The Manor of Llanelen).

Follow a track to the right across the moorland, passing occasional stone cairns to reach the Blorenge summit (1,833 feet). Here is a white trig point and a large cairn which marks the actual summit and provides an impressive view.

Continue along a path on the north east side of the cairn, cutting across the moorland to the north eastern slopes of the hill. Soon you will see below a little square building with radio aerials on its roof. The path descends to this point, which is on the rim of the steep north east escarpment of the Blorenge.

"Good Heavens! must scenes like these expand —
Scenes so magnificently grand —
And millions breathe and pass away
Unbless'd throughout their lithe day,
With one short glimpse."

Such was the emotion felt by the poet, Robert Bloomfield, when he gazed on the landscape stretched out before him when he climbed this hill.

From this point, when the wind direction is suitable, hang glider enthusiasts launch themselves into space for an impressive flight that takes them over the woods above Llanfoist, across high voltage wires, the busy A465 and the fast flowing Usk to land neatly in the Castle Meadows.

Contour around the lip of the escarpment to the left, passing small outcrops of rock. Keep high, enjoying panoramic views up through the Vale of Usk towards Crickhowell, with the mass of the Black Mountains behind. Descend slightly through a shallow gully and follow a 19th century tramroad, contouring around the hillside and leading you back to the starting point at Keeper's Pond.

Grosmont Castle

The Land
of the
Trilateral Castles

"Three castles fayre are in a goodly ground,
Grosmont is one, on a hill it builded was;
Skenfrith the next in a valley it was found,
Whitecastle is the third of worthie fame.
The country round doth bear Whitecastle's name;
A statlie seat, a loftie princlie place,
Whose beauty gives simple soyle some grace."

Thomas Churchyard (1587)

This area can be defined as the land between Abergavenny, Raglan, Monmouth and Pontrilas; bounded by the River Monnow, the A40 and the A465. It contains the sites and remains of several castles, fascinating churches and many ancient manor houses.

ROUTE 7
A WALK ROUND GROSMONT (1 hour)

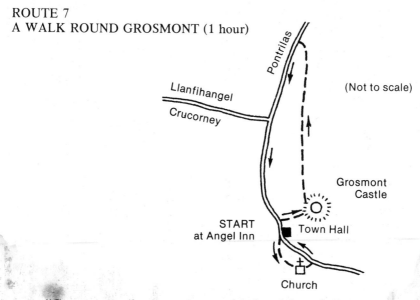

"Grosmont smiles at progress and industrial revolutions.
Its population in 1801 was 519; in 1901 it was 518."

Fred J. Hando

The picturesque village of Grosmont is tucked away on the north east corner of Gwent. It takes it name from a hill to the south (le Gros Mont) known locally as the Graig.

Start from the Angel Inn, Grosmont village (G.R. 404244). Walk down the road and, just beyond the Post Office, turn left up a lane leading to Grosmont Castle. Go through a kissing gate and into the castle grounds.

Overlooking the River Monnow, the castle ruins comprise a keep, curtain walls of the inner ward with angle towers, a massive gatehouse and portions of outer defences. A very striking feature is a 13th century chimney above the remains of the central hall. The original foundations of the castle date from 1070, but the main part of the building is 13th century. The Great Hall on the north side was built in 1210 and it measures 33 yards by 20 yards. Surrounding the castle is a dry moat.

Grosmont Castle was the scene of two dramatic episodes which may be of interest to the visitor. In 1233, Henry III, in a fit of temper, declared that all the Lords Marcher should forfeit their estates. He marched on the border with a motley army of foreign mercenaries and half-trained English, with the aim of enforcing his orders. He captured the town and the castle. But the dispossessed Lords Marcher managed to pursuade their old enemy, Llewelyn the Great, Prince of Gwynydd, to come to their aid. With a body of his fierce Welshmen, they made a sudden attack early one misty morning on Henry's rabble. The King's troops panicked and fled down the Monnow valley.
The story goes that they ran away clad in flimsy nightgowns pursued by mail clad Welshmen bristling with lethal weapons.

Nearly two hundred years later, the then thriving borough of Grosmont was plundered and burnt to the ground after a surprise attack by Owain Glyndwr's second in command, Rhys Gethin (*"the Terrible"*). However, the castle was not captured. Young Harry of Monmouth, the son of Henry IV, was in the neighbourhood with a small army. He collected the Grosmont garison and attacked Gethin's troops while they were celebrating their recent triumph. Henry inflicted a heavy defeat on them and pursued the survivors who eventually re-formed near Brecon, only to be beaten again.

After inspecting the castle ruins (free admission), go back over a metal footbridge and follow the fence around to the right to view the exterior walls. Continue across some fields, keeping parallel to the hedge on the left. Just past a solitary oak tree, turn left through a wooden kissing gate and follow a road to the left. By a junction on the left (Tollstone Way), look out for a small standing stone near the hedge.

Descend towards the large hump of Graig Syfyrddin to reach the old town hall, which surprisingly is dated 1902, but was in fact built in 1832 on the site of a large timbered hall. The town remained a borough until 1860 when it lost the right to appoint two important officials — the Mayor and the Ale Taster. On the ground floor of the Town Hall can be seen the Toll Stone.
Apparently, the first woman to place her basket on this stone on market days used to be allowed trade free of toll. Alternatively, if a man wished to buy from a merchant, he would first place his money on the stone, indicating that the deal was complete.

Another ancient stone can be seen on the side of the road opposite the Town Hall.

Descend the road to the right, past some public toilets. A gabled building on the right was once an inn known as "The Old Duke of York".

Take the lane immediately on the left and shortly turn right through a metal kissing gate into the churchyard (Notice an old bread oven protruding from the wall of a cottage on the right). Look across to the right to see the top of Skirrid Fawr.

The church is surprisingly large, giving some indication of the former importance of the town. It is mainly Early English in design and has a central octagonal tower and spire.

An interesting feature in the grave-yard is the old cross with a crudely carved stone on the top showing the Virgin Mary and Child on one side and the Crucifixion on the other.

Old Stone Cross, Grosmont Churchyard

Go into the chuch and you will immediately feel an atmosphere of antiquity, peace and mustiness. The floor of the now disused nave is well illustrated with engraved stones and there are many interesting tablets to read on the walls. In a corner of the nave can be seen a wooden chest known as the "Grosmont Hutch" and a half finished effigy of a knight, which is reputed to be that of Jack o' Kent who once resided in this corner of Gwent. Numerous stories are told about his deeds and adventures. Some claimed that he was Owain Glyndwr in disguise; others accused him of being a wizard in league with the devil. A legend tells that Jack made a pact with Satan that he should have his soul when he died, whether he was buried inside the church or outside. However, Jack cunningly fooled the devil by arranging for his burial to take place under the very walls of the church at Grosmont, so that he was neither inside nor outside. An old tombstone in the churchyard close to the east wall is said to cover his remains and it is claimed that he died at the age of 120 years. A proverb once used in this neighbourhood would describe someone "as clever as the devil or Jack of Kent".

Leave the church by the main gateway (or over the large stone slab stile on its right — if your legs are long enough!). Turn left and return to your starting point.

"White Castle has all the charm of a story book fortress. The walls follow the line of the prehistoric mound and their colour and curves are reflected on the surface of a deep moat."

Fred J. Hando

ROUTE 8
A WALK TO WHITE CASTLE (3 hours)

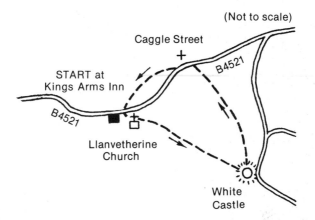

This walk starts from the tiny village of Llanvetherine (Llanwytherin) which is situated on the B4521 about five miles from Abergavenny.

From the King's Arms Inn (G.R. 362172) walk down a lane on the left of this building. Cross a wooden footbridge and go through two wooden gates to enter Llanvetherine churchyard.

The most ancient feature of the church appears to be the tower which has an upper section that projects over the lower part. It contains two bells dated 1582 and 1653. In the chancel can be seen two full size effigies of a former Rector and his wife. They were the Reverend David Powell, who died on 1621, and his wife Mary who is depicted wearing a Welsh hat, her hands clasped as if in prayer. The sculptor for some strange reason placed her feet at right angles to her ankles. It should also be noticed that the wedding ring on the second finger of her right hand would, previous to 1549, have been worn on the fourth finger of the right hand.

Outside, the churchyard slopes gently to the south, where you will find a wooden bridge over a tributary of the river Trothy. On the other side, follow a muddy lane for a short distance. Go through a metal gate on the left and follow a track past a barn. On the hill ahead can be seen the ruins of White Castle. Now through another metal gate and continue following the hedgeline. Cross a brook by a small wooden footbridge. Keep to the right and ahead can be seen another footbridge. Cross over and connect with the Offa's Dyke Long Distance Footpath. Over a stile directly ahead, then straight up a slight rise. On reaching a fence, keep to the left to arrive at another stile. The view is now opening up across to the Blorenge and south to Mynydd Maen.

Cross a stile by a stunted oak and keep right, passing a barn to reach another stile. Keep left, over another stile and follow a lane past castle walls to reach the entrance. Splendid views across to Pen y Gader Fawr and Cat's Back in the Black Mountains.

This well preserved fortress was previously known as Llantilio Castle, standing impressively on this hill about 500 feet above sea level. The present name is supposed to have been derived from its 12th century owner — Gwyn, a prince of Cardigan. In Welsh it was called Castell Gwyn, which meant either White Castle or Gwyn's Castle. Fragments of plaster adhering to the walls also suggest that it was once white-washed.

A romantic story tells how Gwyn lost his castle to a Norman invader and, although old and blind, he fought William Rufus (the Norman) in a dark chamber to even the odds. Gwyn managed to beat his opponent and regain his castle.

It is believed that the castle was originally built by King Stephen in 1184, purely as a military fortress. It is a very good example of a ring castle — the walls are very thick and the outer court, which is protected by lower walls and a complete moat (286 yards in circumference and filled with water), is large enough to contain a small army. In the middle of the 13th century substantial alterations were undertaken. The Keep was demolished and six round towers erected at intervals around the curtain wall. Accommodation for the garrison was probably provided by sheds erected against the internal walls of the inner ward. On the other side of the moat opposite the gateway, a new larger bailey was erected with three round and one rectangular tower. At one time the moat embraced these outer defences as well.

White Castle was held at various times in the 13th century by the powerful famililies of de Burgh and de Braose. Edward I later gave the castle (and its two neighbours) to his brother Edmund "Crouchback", Earl of Lancaster, who improved the castle defences to deal with possible attack by Llewelyn, Prince of Wales. But in 1282 it had lost its importance as a line of defence and in 1320 it was recorded as being derelict. The Duke of Beaufort bought the property in 1825 and it is now in the protection of the Department of the Environment.

One of the main attractions of White Castle is its very situation. It seems remote from the surrounding countryside and the gatehouse tower offers a good view in all directions. A staircase leads up to a wooden platform and from this vantage point can be seen the mountains of Skirrid Fawr, Blorenge, Sugar Loaf, the Black Mountains and Malvern Hills.

Outside the castle, take a track leading from the car park. There is a view to the right of Graig Syfyrddin. Go over a stile and follow a hedge on the right. Then over a stile and continue with a hedge on the right. Observe the old sunken road on the right which was probably once an ancient route to White Castle. Go over a stile on the right and descend to a small footbridge. Then straight on to find a stile in a corner of the field. Turn left and follow the road to Caggle Street. Just past a chapel take a lane leading upwards. Go through a stile (beside a metal gate). Keep to the left of a hedge to reach a stile and then straight on to a stile near a metal water trough. Descend to a small wooden gate just above Llanvetherine church and follow the road back to your starting point.

ROUTE 9
A WALK ROUND SKENFRITH (2 hours)

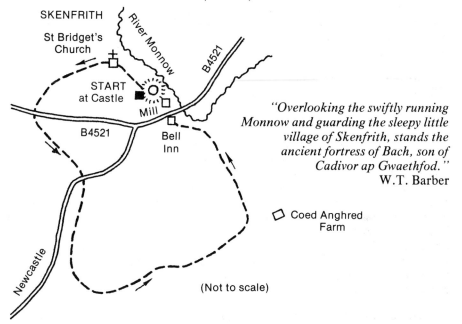

"Overlooking the swiftly running Monnow and guarding the sleepy little village of Skenfrith, stands the ancient fortress of Bach, son of Cadivor ap Gwaethfod."
W.T. Barber

This is a short walk, exploring an ancient castle and church and some of the adjoining countryside. Park in Skenfrith village near The Stores and first make your way to the castle (admission free).

Skenfrith Castle   *18th century engraving*

Situated in this valley by the river Monnow, Skenfrith Castle is overlooked on all sides by higher ground. In such a position it would have been of little strategic value apart from protecting a ford on the Monnow. Security from attack probably depended largely on the swampy nature of the ground surrounding the Castle.

Skenfrith Castle

The name Skenfrith is a corruption of Ynys Cynfraeth. Translated into English this means Cynfraeth's island and probably refers to an area of land flanked on one side by the Monnow and surrounded on the other by swamp. It would seem that Cynfraeth was a chieftain in the 6th century and this was probably the site of his fortified dwelling. In the reign of Henry VIII the village was known as Sgneffroid. Thus it would seem that the castle site was originally an island in the marsh which formed a natural defensive position. Over the years the natural deepening of the river's course probably drained the marsh and left the area surrounding the castle as dry land.

It is a very simple layout for a castle. A circular keep stands on a small mount — the typical Norman construction — and is enclosed by an irregular shaped curtain wall, buttressed at the four corners by round towers. There is a semi-circular bastion on the west side facing the village. The keep was divided into several floors and access to the first one was by a flight of wooden steps.

According to one popular story, Skenfrith Castle and its two neighbouring fortresses were once swopped by King John for three steeds and ten greyhounds! In 1936 the castle was given to the National Trust and it is now looked after by the Department of the Environment.

After exploring the castle, continue up the road to St Bridget's church, which is one of the most interesting churches in Gwent. It has a square tower topped with a wooden lantern-style roof of a design that can frequently be seen in Herefordshire. The church was obviously built for refuge and defence, with narrow slit windows and thick walls. A small carved head of the patron saint — St Bridget — can be seen on the front of the entrance porch.

St Bridget's Church, Skenfrith

The church was probably founded in the 13th century. It has a nave of Norman piers, pointed arches and various styles of windows — Lancet, Decorated and Perpendicular. In the north aisle is the elaborately carved tomb of John ap Phillip Morgan (died 1557), who was the last Governor of the three castles and related to Henry Morgan, the famous pirate. The effigies on his tomb show four men and four women (presumably his children) with every aspect of their elaborate costumes shown in fine detail.

Near this tomb is the Morgan family pew. It is of Jacobean design and about seven feet six inches square. In feudal times, the squire and his family could enjoy the privilege of this draught proof box, whilst the rest of the less fortunate congregation were left to shiver in the cold unheated church.

The greatest treasure of the church is the Skenfrith Cope dating from the 15th century and of red embroidered velvet, depicting the Virgin Mary, saints and angels. It has been suggested that it was possibly embroidered by Queen Eleanor who once stayed at Skenfrith Castle with King Henry III during his campaign against the Welsh.

The Skenfrith Cope

Leaving the church, continue along the road passing the old School House (National School 1843). After approximately 200 yards at a bend in the road, turn left through a metal kissing gate and follow a path across a field to reach a wooden kissing gate and a road. Cross the road and go through a metal gate. Go straight across the field to a metal gate directly opposite. Turn right up the road. Notice the old sunken lane on the left which was the original way. After approximately quarter of a mile, turn sharply left up a cart track which soon provides views over Skenfrith village. Keep following this track through a metal gate.

Next, head for Coed Anghred farm across an open heath. On reaching a metal gate, continue to a point just short of the farm and then descend to a stile in the hedge. Keeping the hedge on your left, make for the river bridge. Cross over the next two stiles to emerge on the road by the Bell Inn.

Cross the road and turn left to follow the grass verge. Observe the old Mill, complete with race and water wheel, on the right. This mill is still in operation and dates back to the 14th century.

It is one of the few remaining working water mills in South Wales and used to roll oats and barley and produce foodstuffs for farm animals fore the present owner bought it in 1947, the mill belonged to the Hilston Par. ate.

Follow the road back to your starting point.

ROUTE 10
IN SEARCH OF DAVY GAM (2 hours)

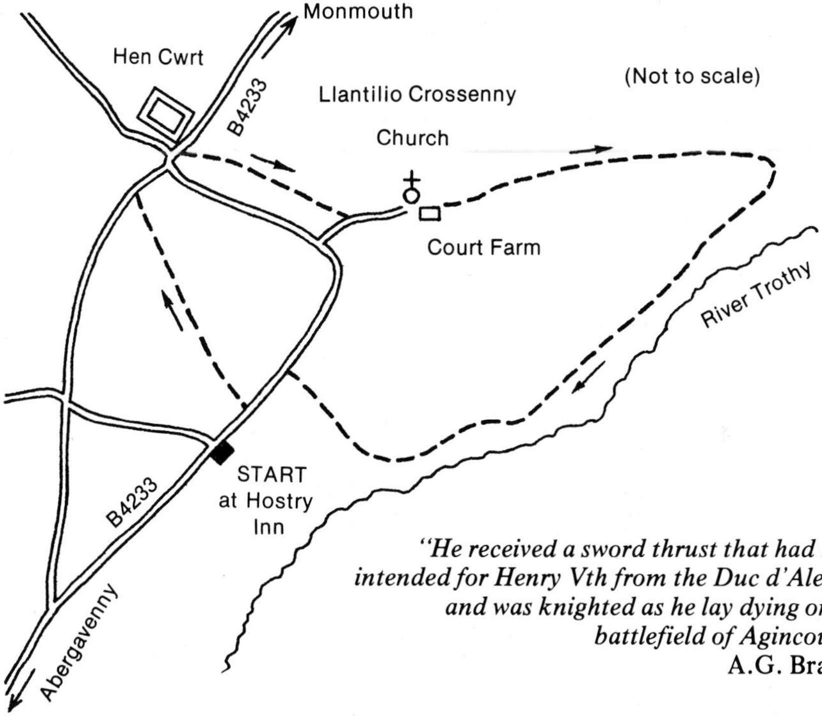

Monmouth

Hen Cwrt

B4233

Llantilio Crossenny

(Not to scale)

Church

Court Farm

River Trothy

B4233

START
at Hostry
Inn

Abergavenny

*"He received a sword thrust that had been
intended for Henry Vth from the Duc d'Alercan
and was knighted as he lay dying on the
battlefield of Agincourt."*
A.G. Bradley

A short walk that explores the vicinity of the fascinating village of Llantilio Crossenny which is situated on the B4223 about six miles east of Abergavenny.

Start from the Hostry Inn (G.R. 396146). According to the sign hanging outside, this inn dates from 1459. It is said to be the second oldest pub in Gwent, the first being the Skirrid Mountain inn, situated about eight miles away as the crow flies. The Hostry sign also depicts the Coat of Arms of David Gam who won fame at the Battle of Agincourt and is believed to have lived in this village at one time.

From the Hostry, walk down the road towards the church steeple. After about 50 yards go through a metal gate on the left by an Offa's Dyke Path sign. Head straight across the field to a stile and the next field to a kissing gate. Turn right and follow the road, taking a turning on the left (signposted 'White Castle'). Shortly a kissing gate on the right gives access to the site of Hen Cwrt (Old Court). Here you will find a rectangular moat full of water lilies, which surrounds a one acre island. At one time, possibly in the 13th century, a manor house stood on this spot owned by the Bishops of Llandaff who held land at Llantilio Crossenny

43

Hen Cwrt, Llantilio Crossenny

In the 15th century it may possibly have been the home of Dafydd ap Llewelyn who was generally referred to as Daffyd Gam because of a cast in one eye. On the eve of the Battle of Agincourt in 1415, he was sent to spy out the strength of the French army. Returning, he gave the brief report, "Enough to be killed, enough to be taken prisoner and enough to run away." He fought bravely during the battle and saved the life of King Henry V at the cost of his own. The grateful king knighted him as he lay dying on the battlefield. It has been suggested that Shakespeare immortalised Daffyd Gam by basing the character of Fluellen (who appeared in several of his historical plays) on this hero of Agincourt.

It is said that Davy Gam had so many children that if they formed a line, hand in hand, they would stretch from Hen Cwrt to the church at Llantilio Crosenny; and like their father they were all cross-eyed!

In later years, Dafydd's son-in-law, William ap Thomas, and his son, William Herbert of Raglan, set up a deer park at Llantilio Crosenny which was in use up until the Civil War. The moated site lay within the deer park. Excavations on the square have shown foundations of a house which was probably built in the 16th century by the Herbert family, but very little evidence of the earlier house was found.

Go back to the road junction. Cross the B4233 and go through a metal kissing gate. Head straight up the field to reach another metal kissing gate by a wall on the left. Follow the edge of a private garden (public right of way) to a third kissing gate.

Some steps leading to the church are now directly ahead. This fine church is built on a raised mound which was once part of an ancient encampment. The locality is the traditional site of a battle between the Saxons and the Welsh (under the leadership of Prince Ynyr) in 546. The prayers of St Teilo, Bishop of Llandaff, turned the tide of battle in favour of the Welshmen, hence the name, "The Church of Teilo — the Coss of Ynyr". It is said that the church was founded in AD 550 on the hillock where the saint prayed during the battle.

The graceful spire of this church is a landmark for many miles around and the annual musical festival held here at Whitsun is to be recommended.

Near the pulpit, the north wall window features Sir David Gam of Llantilio Crosenny "who died in the Battle of Agincourt saving his King".

Three flat stones in the chancel are of special interest. Two of them show figures in Stuart costume and the third is in memory of Vicar Owen Rogers who died in 1660. It shows ten angels' faces, three candles and an inscription:—

> *"I have fought a good fight*
> *I have finished my course*
> *I have kept the faith"*

At the bottom of the stone is another inscription which once read (when legible):—

> *"Here lies a sheapheard late of Christ his sheepe*
> *From sheepe-clothed wolves his lambs did keepe*
> *His monument God's Angels guard and keepe*
> *Til him Th'arkangel wake shall out of sleepe*
> *His soul flown up above the lofty ski.*
> *...IEHOVAH ON HIGH."*

Leave the church and descend the steps at the entrance to the churchyard. Turn left along the road and go through a farmyard (Court Farm) to reach a metal gate at the rear of the building. Go through this gate and down to another metal gate, descend some stone steps and cross a deep entrenchment. Climb the steep bank on the other side and, keeping left of an oak tree, cross the field to reach a kissing gate. Follow the fence on right hand side to reach a stile. Cross the field and head for a metal gate. Now follow a path close to the river Trothy, passing through a very pleasant corner of Gwent.

On reaching a neat, two-arched stone bridge, go across a wooden footbridge on the right, over a tributary of the Trothy. Turn right along road and after approximately 50 yards go through a kissing gate by an Offa's Dyke Path sign. Follow the path beside the stream to reach a wooden footbridge. Cross and turn left to reach a kissing gate and road. Turn left and head for the Hostry Inn.

ROUTE 11
IN SEARCH OF CHARLES ROLLS

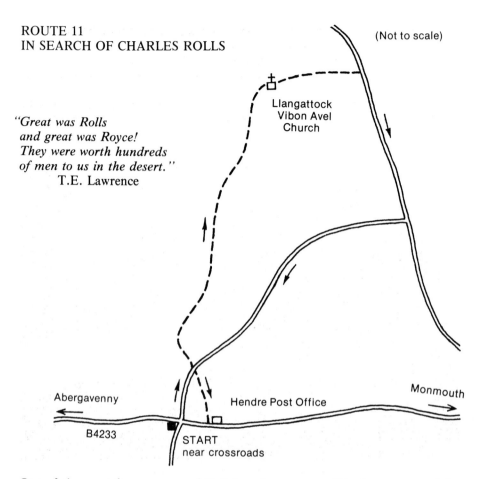

(Not to scale)

Llangattock
Vibon Avel
Church

*"Great was Rolls
and great was Royce!
They were worth hundreds
of men to us in the desert."*
T.E. Lawrence

Abergavenny

B4233

Hendre Post Office

Monmouth

START
near crossroads

One of the most famous men of Britain, whose name still adorns some of the finest cars ever made, lies buried near a ruined church in a quiet corner of Gwent. His grave seems forgotten and known by few. This walk is in memory of Charles Rolls.

Start from the Hendre Post Office which is situated on the B4233 about two miles west of Rockfield. There is a place to park a vehicle on the side of the road leading to Raglan, by a metal gate (G.R. 456146). Follow the road opposite this point, walking north. Shortly a stile will be found on the left, above three stone steps. On the other side, follow a hedge on the right and then cross a wooden footbridge. Now ascend a broad path to reach a rather unnecessary kissing gate which can be passed on either side. The path passes above a wooded dingle to a metal gate, followed by a kissing gate. It then contours neatly around the gently sloping hillside above Darlin Wood. Ahead can be seen the little church of Llangattock Vibon-Avel.

The tall granite cross in the churchyard is a war memorial to the men of this parish who fell in both world wars. Unfortunately the church is in a very dilapidated and unsafe condition and is always locked. It contains some fine memorials to members of the Rolls family and a private family pew on the south side of the chancel.

There is an interesting inscription in the porch relating to the charities of the parish of Llangattock Vibon Avel (more correctly — Llangattwg Feibon Afel) but far too lengthy to relate here!

Charles Stewart Rolls preparing for a flight

To find the grave of Charles Stewart Rolls, go to the eastern corner of the graveyard, just below Llangattock Manor which stands close to the church. The grave of this famous Englishman is topped by a Celtic style cross and bears the inscription:—

> *"Blessed are the pure in heart*
> *for they shall see God."*

He is placed in line with five other members of the Rolls family who have slightly smaller Celtic style crosses above them.

Charles Rolls was born in 1877, the son of John Alan Rolls, first Lord of Llangattock. At the age of 18 years, Charles bought his first car and was one of the first three people in Wales to own one. He began manufacturing them a few years later and was joined in his new business venture by Henry Royce in 1904. The firm soon prospered and in 1907 a Rolls Royce car created a world record for reliability.

Charles was also a keen balloonist and made 170 ascents using gas from Monmouth gas works which he obtained by a special arrangement. In due course he followed the example of the American Wright brothers and took up flying aeroplanes. He formed the Aero Club in 1903 and won the Gordon Bennet Gold Medal that year for the longest time spent in the air in a single flight. His greatest flying achievement was to cross the English Channel in 95 minutes, which was a faster time than Bleriot took. He also accomplished the first return journey without landing until the end of the flight.

Unfortunately his brief, but eventful, life finished a few months later when he was killed in an aircraft crash at Bournemouth, caused by the collapse of his tailplane. This tragic event gave him the rather dubious honour of becoming the first Englishman to be killed in an aircraft crash.

The next section of this route is mainly road walking. Otherwise, return by the outward journey.

Go through a lychgate at the rear of the church and then ascend to a wooden gate; over a cattle grid and follow the driveway to reach a road. Turn right, passing the lodge house of Llangattock Manor. Take the next turning on the right; a narrow lane descending and providing good views of the Hendre Estate. This large brick and stone Tudor mansion was built in the early 19th century and was later the main home of the Rolls family.

At the bottom of the hill the road crosses a stream. Immediately on the other side go through a metal kissing gate on the left. After passing through a small copse, cross a metal bridge to shortly pass through a wooden gateway by the Hendre Post Office and near a drinking trough inscribed:—

1894
Pure Life

Pure Water

Charles Rolls was perhaps a man ahead of his time. His life was short but, in association with Royce, his name lives on as a symbol of engineering perfection.

He undoubtedly helped to bring true the prophetic words of Roger Bacon, a Franciscan monk, written over 600 years ago:—

> *"We will be able to construct machines which will propel large ships with greater speed than whole garisons of rowers and we will need only one pilot; we will be able to propel carriages with incredible speed without the assistance of any animal; and we will be able to make machines which by means of wings will enable us to fly through the air like birds."*

The Western Valleys

"Over in the west are rows and rows of depressing dwellings where miners live; their children play in shabby streets; the wheels at the pit heads revolve pitilessly as men go to work in the dark underworld of dead forests, and when they come up again it is to look upon the black monstrous, menacing slag heaps rearing their hideous heads everywhere."

W.J. Smart
"Where Wye and Severn flow"

Nantyglo   *19th century engraving*

A fascinating area, avoided by many who think of these valleys as an area still scarred by slag heaps. In actual fact most of the industrial scars have now been removed. The valleys give access to fine ridge walks, with extensive and spectactular views. They contain wooded cwms, industrial curiosities, old churches, and provide an experience unique to this corner of Wales.

Before the period of the Industrial Revolution, Wales had remained a pastoral and agricultural area, with its small towns serving as centres of local trade and its population fairly evenly distributed between North and South Wales.

In about 1750 experienced ironworkers from Staffordshire and the North of England began to establish ironworks in the hilly areas of South East Wales where supplies of iron ore, limestone, and coal were readily available.

The first area to be developed was a narrow strip of hill country stretching about twenty miles east and west of Blaenavon (Gwent) to Hirwaun (Mid Glamorgan). This area became for some years the most important iron making region in Britain. From this early industry developed the need for better communications, resulting in canals, tram roads and railways. In due course the iron industry, which depended on coal for smelting, came to be overshadowed by the South Wales coal industry.

The area was rapidly converted from a land of wooded valleys with sparkling clear rivers to one of the most concentrated centres of British industry. People seeking work came in their thousands from the rural areas of Wales, England and Ireland, attracted by the possibility of employment or higher wages.

Houses were built by the ironmasters and mine owners for their workers. They generally consisted of two storeys built in terraces of twenty to fifty dwellings along the contours of the steep hillsides. These small communities grew into towns, such as Ebbw Vale and Nantyglo. In 1801 (the date of the first National Census), 45,000 people lived in Gwent and by 1851 this figure had reached 157,000.

Today, most of the coal mines have closed, as have great steelworks such as Ebbw Vale. When production ceased here in 1978 it marked the end of an era of 200 years of iron and steel making in the Western Valleys of Gwent.

Many of the coal tips have been removed and derelict sites landscaped. The valleys of Gwent are now proving attractive to visitors, particularly those with an interest in Britain's industrial past. But western Gwent is perhaps surprisingly rural for an area which once contained so much industry. As good walking country, extending for many miles, it has a special appeal.

ROUTE 12
THE DEVIL'S BRIDGE
AND THE LONELY SHEPHERD
(Short route 2½ hours,
Long route 3½ hours)

"One of the most romantic dells
it is possible to imagine,
terminated by the truly striking
Waterfall of Pwll-y-Cwn."
John White (1877)

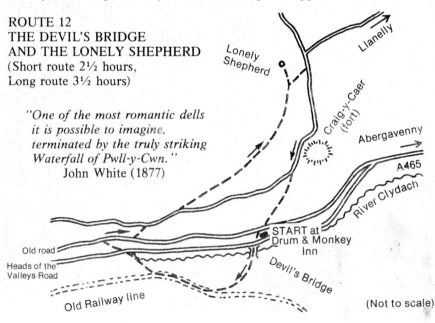

A walk exploring the limestone scenery of the Clydach Gorge and the south eastern slopes of Mynydd Llangattock.

Start from the Drum and Monkey Inn (G.R. 216125), which is situated near Blackrock on the side of the old road from Gilwern to Brynmawr which runs parallel to and above the A465 Heads of the Valleys road through the Clydach Gorge.

From the inn, go through a gate and then a subway passing under the Heads of the Valleys road. Turn right and go through a metal gate, down a flight of steps into the depths of the gorge, to reach the Devil's Bridge.

The Devil's Bridge, Clydach Gorge

Below the bridge a waterfall tumbles into the narrow chasm below. With a little imagination you may see the face of the devil in a rock on the left which apparently provides the reason for the bridge's name.

The pool below the waterfall is known as Pwll-y-Cwn which signifies the "Pool of Dogs". It is said that a fox, in order to escape from a pack of hounds, once jumped down the cascade and was followed by the dogs who were stunned by the fall and all drowned.

Above the bridge is Cwm Pwcca where the fairies are said to dwell and it is locally claimed that William Shakespeare once visited this location which provided inspiration for his play "A Midsummer Night's Dream".

On the other side of the bridge, ascend a flight of steps to pass above a picturesque side valley on the right. The steps peter out and you ascend a long steep slope to reach some stone steps by a cottage. At the top, turn right, passing ruined cottages, to pass on the right the twin tunnel mouths of the old Abergavenny to Brynmawr railway. There are fine views from here looking down the Clydach Gorge to Skirrid Fawr in the distance. Following a path beside the old railway line, you will soon pass the remains of Gellifelin station with its rotting wooden platforms and brick shelters.

Carry on beside the old line, passing under pylon wires, to reach a stile on the left. Then turn right and immediately go over another stile and shortly another stile — on to a gate and past an old lime kiln to reach a road. Turn right and then straight on at the next track junction, through a wooden kissing gate to follow a gravel path downwards between trees into the Cwm Clydach Nature Reserve. Descend to a wooden gate and turn right down some steps to pass through a subway beneath the Heads of the Valleys road. Keep right and follow a tarmac path to a gate. Soon you will see (after heavy rain) an impressive waterfall on the right. A track gives access for a closer inspection of the fall. (This is a good spot for a lunch stop).

Continue up the tarmac path to find a track on the right (by a manhole cover!) ascending steeply to the old Clydach road above. Turn right along the pavement, passing a derelict garage. To complete the SHORT WALK follow the road back to start, or otherwise continue in search of the Lonely Shepherd.

Go past a second garage (Hafod) to turn left through a metal gate along a wide track to join another road. Turn right and follow this road for about half-a-mile, passing Hafod farm. About 30 yards past a cattle grid take a path on the left leading across country. (Good mountain navigation experience necessary, particularly in poor visibility). Cross a small stream and proceed in a north easterly direction, passing near a stone wall, across a stream, and over another stream. The route is quite well trodden, but other tracks make the way confusing.

An old tram road is joined by a very rocky area which contours around the hillside providing views down the Vale of Usk to Abergavenny. Ignore a path descending to the right and take the middle of three tracks at the next junction. (The right hand one ends at a cliff edge — take care not to follow it!). Follow the middle track for a short way and then go over a hump on the right and steeply downhill through a gap in some cliffs to "The Lonely Shepherd". This pillar of limestone, standing on the edge of the escarpment, is according to legend a shepherd who was turned into stone for ill treating his wife. However, on Midsummer night he comes to life and descends into the valley to search for his spouse.

The Lonely Shepherd

After inspecting the stone shepherd and the fine view from this location, follow with care a narrow path back along the edge of an old quarry (to the south) to reach a path leading diagonally back under the quarry face with the Lonely Shepherd standing above. The path then zig-zags downwards to join the road below (by the junction to Llanelly).

Turn right along the road and follow it for about three-quarters of a mile to reach a point above Craig-y-Caer (a limestone "tower" below on the site of an Iron Age hill fort). Carry on along the road and just before a bend turn left and descend to a wooden pylon; turn right beneath the wires and follow a track down into the valley, passing derelict quarries (following a line of poles), to reach a metal gate. Finally rejoin the old Blackrock road by the Old Drum and Monkey Inn.

ROUTE 13
IN SEARCH OF
IESTYN MORTIMER

(3½ hours)

(Not to scale)

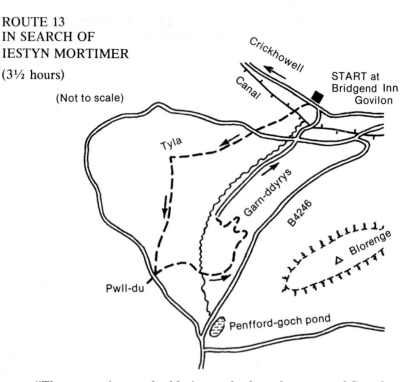

START at
Bridgend Inn
Govilon

"The mountain was shuddering to the forge-hammers of Garndyrus, and faintly on the wind came the plaintive singing of the Irish haulers. Llanfoist farms were sleeping in the pit-blackness below, their blind windows winking at the stars..."

Alexander Cordell
"Rape of the Fair Country"

For those who have read Alexander Cordell's famous novel, the title and route of this walk will have a special meaning. Iestyn Mortimer was the hero of this book and the story was woven around the life and times of the people who worked at the Garn-ddyrus ironworks and lived in a tiny village of that name on the eastern slopes of the Blorenge mountain.

Start from the Bridgend Inn at Govilon (G.R. 265138). Turn left and go up Church Lane to pass beneath a stone archway below the canal. On the other side of the arch ascend a narrow flight of steps on the left to reach a stile. Go through a field beside the canal and then head up to the right following an old incline to reach a metal gate and tarmac lane. Turn right up the road, bear left at the next junction and cross a bridge over the old Abergavenny to Merthyr railway line.

Follow a tarmac lane, ascending gradually the west side of Cwm Llanwenarth, for about 1½ miles to reach Llwyn-y-Celyn farm. Go through a metal gate and past the farm, following a metalled road to the right. Look out for a small well on the left. About 50 yards beyond this well, turn left up a rough track where you can enjoy fine views across to the Black Mountains, Sugar Loaf, Skirrid Fawr and Abergavenny.

Ascend for some distance to reach the 400-ft contour line where you join Hill's Tramroad near Tyla quarry. Turn left and follow this stony track contouring around the hillside. This track was constructed in about 1848 by Thomas Hill to link the Tyla quarry with Garn-ddyrys ironworks and, by a series of inclines, to the Brecon and Abergavenny canal at Llanfoist.

Look across the valley to the left to see a well defined terraced area with a few ruined cottages on the hillside below. This is the site of Garn-ddyrys village.

The old tram road contours around the head of the cwm with an impressive drop below to the valley floor. At the head of Cwm Llanwenarth, on a flat piece of ground, stands a large white building which was once used as a village hall by the community of Pwll-du. It is now used as an Adventure Centre and very little remains to be seen of this one time mining community as the village was demolished in 1966. Most people find it sad to think that this was once a thriving community, complete with brass band. In the 1880's some of its members emigrated to Pennsylvania, U.S.A., and set up a new band which exists to this day and is known as the Pwlldu Brass Band.

At a junction of tracks, leave the gravel path and go across a stile in a stone wall (constructed from old tram rails). Carry on to an iron kissing gate and beyond to reach a road. Near here is a stone archway. This was the entrance to the Pwll Du tunnel (built in 1815) which at three miles long and lined with stone was the longest tramroad tunnel in Britain, allowing the trams to go through the hillside and emerge near the Blaenavon ironworks.

Go left for approximately 250 yards and then left by a footpath sign (Govilon 3.3 km) along a gravel track. The cottage below used to be the Lamb Inn of Pwll-du which closed in 1958.

Head down to a wooden gate near the cottage and then follow a path between stone walls to a metal gate. Go through this gate and the one ahead. Turn right, walking parallel to a hedge and beside the remains of an old stone wall to enter a narrow cutting. Just beyond the low stone wall (across the cutting) is a cave entrance on the right, known as Black Cavern. Unfortunately the roof is very unstable, so do not enter.

The next section of the path is rather dangerous for the tramroad has collapsed. It continues as a narrow path above steep limestone cliffs. If you are not happy about making the airy traverse, go back to the cutting and go over the top to reconnect with the tramroad on the other side. (Particularly advisable if you are walking with young children).

Cross a stile on the other side and follow a stone wall on the left. The broad tramroad continues above steep cliffs with the track curving around into a gully, in places supported by stone walls which are standing the test of time very well, except where it crosses a stream tumbling down a gulley. Here, the old bridge has disappeared or collapsed. Observe the cliffs of intricately weathered limestone on the right. Also notice regular stones with holes bored into them which once carried tram rails.

Below is a heap of black slag, resembling an enormous pig, which marks the site of the Garn-ddyrys ironworks. It opened in about 1814 and at its peak it turned out about 300 tons per week of iron bars, rails and plates which were taken down on Hill's tramroad to the Brecon and Abergavenny canal at Llanfoist for transport to Newport. From there the products were sent to many parts of Britain and exported to places throughout the world.

The ironworks closed in about 1864 when operations were transferred to a new works at Blaenavon (Forgeside). Today, all that is left of Garn-ddyrys ironworks is this huge pile of slag and the remains of a section of tramroad tunnel (G.R. 257119) which was an artificial tunnel probably constructed to protect the trams from flying slag.

Slag from Garn-ddyrys Forge

Descend to this black heap and below it follow a path leading down into the valley. The track helter skelters down to the ruined remaining houses of Garn-ddyrys. In its heyday in the 1840's it boasted two pubs: The Queen and the Puddler's Arms, and a boisterous place it must have been, resembling an American township in the Mid West in pioneer days. In 1851 it was recorded that about 300 people lived near the Garn-ddyrys ironworks.

Go through a metal gate and down through fields passing ruined cottages. On past tumbling stone walls and down through the trees in this delightful valley with the noise of a tumbling stream singing in your ears to reach Bryn-y-Cwm farm.

Through a gate and left down the farm drive to reach a road. Turn right along the road through the bottom of Cwm Lanwenarth, passing old cottages and farmhouses. Keep straight on at road junction and then shortly go left over a bridge crossing an old railway track. Turn right down Station Road. Pass over the Brecon and Abergavenny canal and immediately turn left down a narrow alley near the Canal Bank Stores. Cross a road and down another alley, directly opposite, to join a road. Turn left over a bridge to reach your starting point.

N.B. Alexander Cordell spells the name as Garndyrus and Ordnance Survey give it as Garn-ddyrys.

ROUTE 14
WHISTLE FOR A RACEHORSE (2½ hours)

(Not to scale)

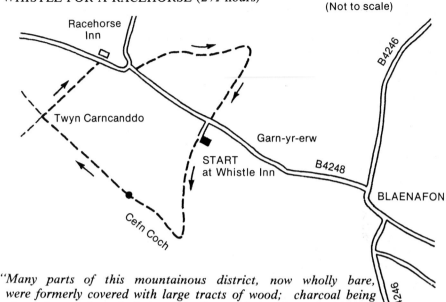

"Many parts of this mountainous district, now wholly bare, were formerly covered with large tracts of wood; charcoal being the only species of fuel originally used in the operation of smelting, both in the bloomeries and furnaces."

Archdeacon William Coxe (1801)

A mountain walk taking in two inns and very suitable for thirsty walkers! Start from the Whistle Inn (G.R. 229101). This is situated just beyond Garn-yr-ew to the north west of Blaenavon and off the B4248 road to Brynmawr.

From the inn, follow a tarmac road towards Coity Mountain, passing a cottage on the right. Go over a ditch and up to a metal gate to follow a track ascending the hillside to the crest of the ridge. On gaining the top of the ridge turn right to walk in a north westerly direction. Extensive views may be enjoyed across to the Black Mountains, Sugar Loaf and Skirrid Fawr. To the west is the adjoining valley of Cwmtillery and Mynydd James.

Follow the ridge to the broad plateau of Cefn Coch over very tufty ground. Ahead, the Brecon Beacons may come into view. Continue along the ridge for another mile-and-a-half and descend its northern end to reach Twn Carncanddo — a small standing stone on the right of the track. Follow a path to the right, heading in the direction of the Sugar Loaf and, later, down beside a ditch carrying a stream. Then branch off to the left towards a slate roofed building (Race Horse Inn, G.R. 216112). Go over a stile and across the road to the inn.

From the Race Horse Inn follow the B4248 towards Blaenavon and shortly cross an old railway track, now covered with tarmac. Near here once stood Waun Afon station which, when in use, was the highest railway station in England and Wales (standard gauge). It was situated at an altitude of 1,400 ft or 427 m above sea level. It was closed to passengers on 5th May 1941 and closed entirely on 23rd June 1954.

Follow a road on the left (road to Daren-felin) and, opposite a telephone box, climb a track leading behind some grass covered spoil heaps. Here is an extensive view across a man-shaped landscape towards the Black Mountains.

At the end of the spoil heaps, where the track becomes a concrete road, turn right, go past a rubbish tip and continue down to the road, not far from the Whistle Inn.

ROUTE 15
CWM SYCHAN (2½ hours)

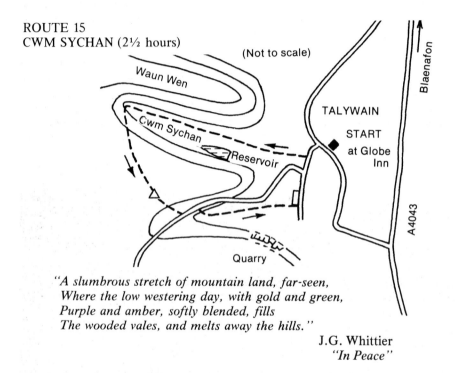

"A slumbrous stretch of mountain land, far-seen,
Where the low westering day, with gold and green,
Purple and amber, softly blended, fills
The wooded vales, and melts away the hills."

J.G. Whittier
"In Peace"

Start from the Globe Inn at Talywain (G.R. 260043) which is alongside the B4246. Follow the road opposite the inn (The British Road) and after approximately 200 yards turn right following a lane signposted to Castle Wood.

On reaching a fork (near a stream) go left to follow a cart track past old mine workings and bear right to reach a metal gate in the corner of a fence and a bridlepath sign. Go through the gate and follow the path to the left, passing below the ruins of a building (known as the Newfoundout) silhouetted against the sky.

Soon you are looking down on a reservoir in the valley below. The fence ends; cross a stream and keep straight on, following a line of fence posts. You are now in the upper part of a beautiful and peaceful valley with the only sounds coming from the birds and the sheep.

58

The track becomes a ditch beside the remains of an old stone wall and soon descends into the valley. Turn left by an isolated fence post and head down towards the valley floor. Then turn right along a well defined path ascending gently to the head of the valley, where the track bears left and ascends to the crest of the ridge. At this point, turn left to reach an iron marker post. Continue left along a wide track with Cwm Sychan on the left to pass another iron marker post.

Ahead can be seen Twm Barlwm. Fifty yards after the marker post, bear left at a division of tracks to follow a wide, rutted track along the middle of the ridge. Magnificent views into the Abertillery valley can be enjoyed on the right, down to Llanhilleth. On the ridge beyond, Pen-y-Fan Pond may be seen glinting in the sunlight, which incidently is the highest Country Park in Wales. Looking back, the Brecon Beacons may be seen.

A trig' point is reached (G.R. 238035) at an altitude of 1,597 feet (488 metres). From here, head straight across in a south easterly direction, following a wide track to reach a road. Turn left and descend into Cwm Bwrgwm. Shortly, a wide grass verge appears on the right hand side of the road to follow high above a v-shaped valley, unfortunately spoilt by rubbish dumping. By a house (on the left), leave the road and descend a few yards to follow a grass track on the right leading down into the broader valley.

Derelict cottages at The British above Abersychan

Ahead is the Pontypool—Blaenavon railway line with the largest horse-shoe bend in Britain. Across to the right can be seen the Cwm-byrgwm balance winding gear. This is the only one in South Wales that still remains in its original position (i.e. it has not been removed to a museum).

Follow the track down to a stile in a fence. Below and ahead are the ruined terraced cottages of The British Village which once housed the workers who spent their days toiling at the British Ironworks. Like the homes that once formed the mining community, the ironworks have now disappeared into oblivion.

Continue down the path, past the last row of cottages to join a gravel track. Turn left and then right on meeting a road. This will lead you back to the starting point. ('The cottages at The British are to be restored).

ROUTE 16
CWMTILLERY CIRCUIT (3 hours)

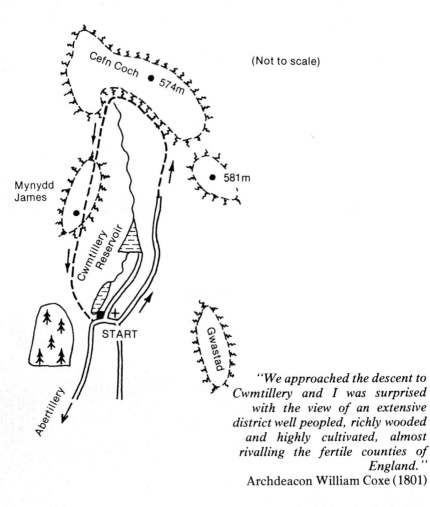

(Not to scale)

"We approached the descent to Cwmtillery and I was surprised with the view of an extensive district well peopled, richly wooded and highly cultivated, almost rivalling the fertile counties of England."
Archdeacon William Coxe (1801)

From Abertillery, follow a road on the north side of the town leading up to Cwmtillery Reservoir. Park on the side of the road, by the first lake (G.R. 218062). From the lake, walk back a few yards to the Cwmtillery road and follow the pavement to the left. Ascend a short hill and just around the corner take a turning on the left to follow a road just above the Parish Church of St Paul. As you gradually climb the side of the valley, you will be able to enjoy good views across the reservoir.

Some distance beyond the reservoir the road steepens. Just before a dip, turn right up a cart track. This climbs to the rim of the valley. Follow a path beside a long stone wall. A few hundred yards above the end of the stone wall, the track drops into the head of the valley (below Cefn Coch) and ascends the other side, cutting across the upper slopes of Mynydd James. Keep on the rim of the slope, looking down into Cwm Tyleri. (In summer the track is easily lost when the ferns are high).

Opposite the dam of the reservoir, follow the path keeping to the right of a land drain (open stone-lined gulley). Go over a stile and down to join a concrete path. Ahead is the sprawling town of Abertillery.

Cwmtillery Colliery was sunk in 1850 and the population of Abertillery then was about 8,000. Rates were about 2s. 4d. in the £ and coal cost 13s. a ton.

At one time Abertillery was famous for its quarries which supplied stone for the construction of Newport docks. Above Geli Crug, the Blackstone quarries in the early part of the 19th century produced the finest material for tombstones.

It is of interest that Archdeacon Coxe on his third tour of Gwent in 1797 referred to this area as *"one seldom visited except for grouse shooting"* and the land *"as richly wooded, highly cultivated and abounding with romantic scenery"*.

Follow the concrete path down to the starting point.

Looking towards Cwmtillery

ROUTE 17
NANT GWYDDON FACH (1—1½ hours)

"Possibly one of the loveliest places near to Abercarn is the Gwyddon valley which is renowned for its natural charm."
Official Guide to Abercarn (1947)

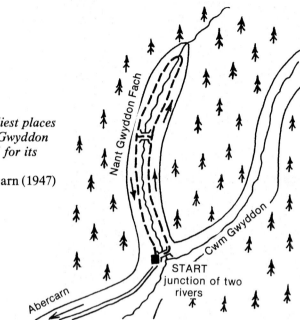

An easy walk for young toddlers or the elderly. From Abercarn follow the Gwyddon valley to reach a point where the valley divides. Here is a parking area near the junction of two rivers (G.R. 237959).

Ebbw Forest is part of the 13th century Forest of Machen which was gradually destroyed by man's need for bark for leather tanning, charcoal for iron-smelting and wood for pit props in the coal mines. Today the forest comprises mainly spruce, larch and pine planted by the Forestry Commission in this century.

It was once planned to build blast furnaces in this valley in 1836 by the Monmouthshire Iron and Coal Company who had leased an extensive area of land from Sir Benjamin Hall (who later became Lord Llanover). However the Company was later ruined by a sudden drop in iron prices and the scheme was abandoned.

The following route is a short, fairly level walk, particularly suitable for small children or elderly folk who do not want to go far. The first part of the route is entirely on tracks with a firm surface and the walk may be extended into the upper part of the valley. This involves a narrow path which can be wet in places, but is fairly level and easy going.

Nant Gwyddon Fach

Go over the bridge and turn left over a stile to follow a forestry track near the river. This is pleasant, level walking, accompanied by a babbling brook, birdsong, the scent of pine trees and an impressive tree-scape. Through a gate, the track rises gently. On reaching a clearing where the valley narrows, you may turn left over the stream and return to the starting point down the other bank (total distance approximately 2 miles).

The more energetic will continue on the right hand bank. Soon you are in a very attractive valley with a bare hillside ahead. At the end of the valley the trees are less dominant; you are left with the hills, the stream and the sheep. Go down to a stile, cross the stream and turn left along a narrow path on the other side.

A stile is reached; continue beside the rushing stream with the high tree covered slopes closing in on you once more. On reaching the junction (previously mentioned), the track broadens. Continue to a gate, go over a stile, and you are back at the starting point.

This short walk provides just a taste of this magnificent area. Longer and more exacting walks may be planned with the aid of a map. The one recommended is Ordnance Survey 1:25,000 Second Series Sheet ST 29/39 (Cwmbran).

CWMCARN SCENIC FOREST DRIVE

In the next valley to the south is a 7 mile car drive through mountain forest which provides extensive views of the Bristol Channel and Brecon Beacons. The facilities include picnic sites, adventure play areas, forest and mountain walks. The Scenic Drive is managed by the Forestry Commission and is open from Easter to August (11 a.m. — 8 p.m.) and from September to October (11 a.m. — 6 p.m.)

ROUTE 18
TWM BARLWM (Correctly Twyn Barllwm)

(3 hours)

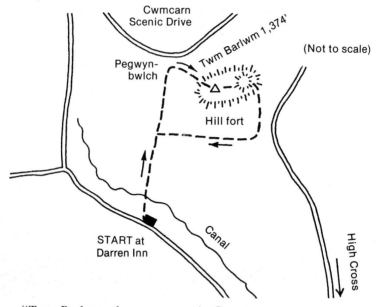

*"Twm Barlwm, that green pap in Gwent
With its dark nipple in a cloud."*

W.H. Davies

Start from the Darren Inn (G.R. 234914) on the side of the A467 in Risca. Follow Darren Road and ascend a narrow and attractive valley. Ahead will be seen the pass of Pegwyn-bwlch. Go through a gate and the path becomes a grass and gravel track. Down below is a small brick bungalow, known as Hanson's Lodge.

On gaining the top of the pass one reaches the Cwmcarn Scenic Drive and fine views looking down into the wooded valley of Cwm Carn.

Follow a well worn path to the right up the grass covered slopes to reach the summit of Twm Barlwm. This is the southern climax of the ridge of Mynydd Maen which stretches from Pontypool to Risca. On the summit of Twm Barlwm at 1,374 feet is the site of an ancient encampment, protected by an elliptical ditch. It is the highest Iron Age hill fort in Gwent and also the most prominent. At the north eastern end is a massive mound, which unfortunately over the years has partially collapsed and has been mutilated by motorcycle scramblers. This mound is by legend reputed to be the burial mound of an ancient British Chieftain. Some historians believe that it was thrown up by the Normans as a Motte and Bailey timber castle and it is marked as such on the Ordnance Survey map.

Archdeacon Coxe came here in 1801 and described his visit as follows:-

"... about two miles from the village of Henllys, we quitted our chase, and rode up a gentle acclivity, clothed with copses and underwood, along a narrow stoney path and in three quarters of an hour reached the bottom of the swelling hill called Twyn Barlwm. We skirted its base over some heather and boggy ground and alighting from our horses ascended to the top.

"... Twyn Barlwm situated on the highest point of the chain which bounds the rich valleys watered by the Usk, commands one of the most singular and glorious prospects I have yet enjoyed in Monmouthshire; and which cannot be reduced to a specific and adequate description."

Mynydd	14	Twm Barlwm
Machen	Locks	from Alt-yr-yn

From the mound, which is generally referred to by Newport folk as "the pimple", descend on the south east side, following a path down to the edge of a forestry plantation. On joining the road below, turn right and follow it for a short distance. Bear right by a fence, following a grass track.

Cross a rutted track and keep straight on, following the fence to reach a wooden stile in the corner of a field. Go over the stile and keep the fence on your left. Turn left by a "Public Footpath" sign to follow path through some fields. Go over a stile and continue beside the fence. From here is a view over Risca toward Mynydd Machen. The track descends to a stile and down to some farm buildings which are the remnants of Darren farm. Turn right here to reach a gate and continue along a forest track shortly to rejoin the earlier route. Turn left on to a gravel track and descend to the Darren Inn.

"To many a son of Gwent, exiled in distant lands, home thoughts conjure up a vision of a skyline, long and nobly undulating, with a strange tump towards the left, upheld by a bare mountain shoulder. The vision appears usually in sunset colours, with the hill pale mauve against a sunset sky."

Fred J. Hando
"Rambles in Gwent" (1924)

ROUTE 19
PANT YR EOS — *THE VALLEY OF THE NIGHTINGALE* (3 hours)

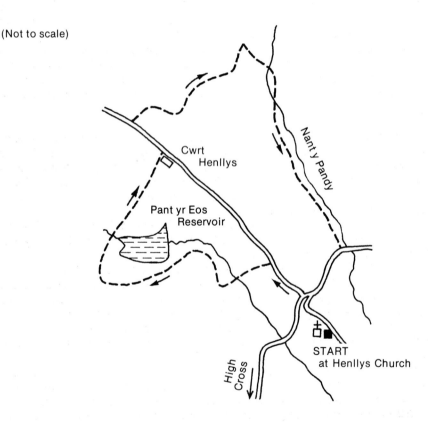

(Not to scale)

Cwrt Henllys

Pant yr Eos Reservoir

Nant y Pandy

START at Henllys Church

High Cross

"The lanes of Gwent have a magic of their own in the daylight, but this magic is increased a hundredfold under the light of a July moon."

E. Elliot Stock

Start from Henllys church (approximately 3 miles north of Rogerstone at G.R. 266910). Park outside the church gates and walk back a few yards to the road. Turn left following the road towards Twm Barlwm. Keep straight on at the junction. Turn left over a stile (opposite a small layby). Keep high across the field to reach a stile by a metal gate. Then keeping the fence on your right, descend to a stream and small footbridge.

Cross a stile and keep straight on through the wood. On reaching a broader path, turn right and continue through a dense wood to reach a stile. Turn right along a cart track. Soon you are below the dam of Pant yr Eos reservoir and ascending a very pleasant path to pass above the left hand side of the reservoir. A peaceful spot with views across to the "pimple" of Twm Barlwm.

At the end of the wood go over a stile and cross the field to a line of trees at the end of the field ahead. Turn right here and descend, passing just above the western end of the reservoir. Cross the feeder stream with its settling ponds and on to a metal gate, now following a wide cart track.

As you gently climb, look to the right to see Henllys church below and the Ridgeway beyond. Pass through a metal gate on the left, keeping left of a barn to pass behind Cwrt Henllys farm and through a metal gate to reach a road.

Either turn right here to walk directly back to Henllys church or turn left for a longer walk...

Follow the road to the left to reach a bend and turn right here, over a stile by a footpath sign (Castell-y-Bwch 3 kms). Follow a metalled surface for approximately 200 yards, enjoying the extensive views. Go right, over a stile by a metal gate and down a grass lane between hedges to reach another metal gate. Carry on for a few yards and turn left, keeping the hedge on your left, bearing right (slightly) to reach a pylon.

Go over a stile and down to a hedge below. Turn right following the hedge down to a stream. Cross over and keep right along a cart track. By Pandy Mawr farm (dated 1719), turn left through a metal gate.

Follow the farm drive, go across a stream, through a metal gate and turn right at the junction of two tracks, re-crossing the stream, past some stables and down to a gap in the hedge in the bottom left hand corner of the field. Cross the stream and turn right to reach a stile. Keep the stream on your right and go through a holly grove to reach a footbridge. Cross it and then go over a stile and turn left to follow a hedge to find a stile in the corner of the field, above a ditch (acrobatics necessary to cross it!).

Keep the hedge on your left and walk through a copse to reach a stile just above the stream. Walk on beside conifers to reach a stile at the end of the wood. Cross a stream and, keeping the hedge on your left, make for a metal gate ahead. Go straight across the next field and through the left of two gates by a cottage. Down to a road, turn right and go through the second of two metal gates on the left. Head over a hump in a field to see Henllys church directly ahead. Go through a metal gate and directly across the next field to a metal gate by Church Farm to reach the starting point at Henllys church.

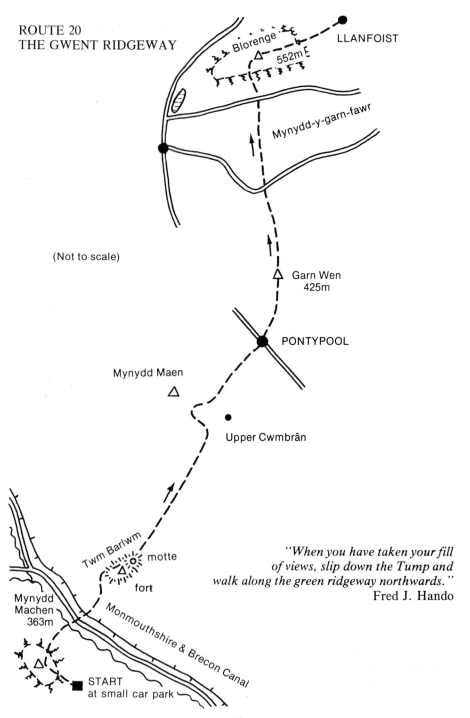

ROUTE 20
THE GWENT RIDGEWAY

LLANFOIST

Blorenge

552m

Mynydd-y-garn-fawr

(Not to scale)

Garn Wen
425m

PONTYPOOL

Mynydd Maen

Upper Cwmbrân

Twm Barlwm   motte

fort

Mynydd
Machen
363m

Monmouthshire & Brecon Canal

START
at small car park

*"When you have taken your fill
of views, slip down the Tump and
walk along the green ridgeway northwards."*
Fred J. Hando

A linear route which can be walked in two sections or, depending on your fitness, as one complete walk.

Section I — Mynydd Machen to Pontypool Park (5 hours)

Start from a small parking area on the south east side of Mynydd Machen (G.R. 231897). Follow an obvious path to the summit of the hill, which is an excellent viewpoint. Descend to the road below and follow it down through the woods to cross a Forestry Commission road. On reaching an isolated cottage, follow a grass track (on the right of the cottage) to reach a bend in the road at the bottom of the hill, where there is a junction of tracks. Keep straight on and shortly descend some steps leading to the old Sirhowy railway line.

Cross the railway track and turn right along a road to shortly cross the Afon Ebbw on a stone bridge and follow Black Vein Road. On reaching the A467 go across and turn right to follow the pavement. Then turn left up Melart Street to reach a metal kissing gate. After crossing three stiles, turn right to follow a wire fence to reach the canal towpath. Follow this to the second stone bridge over the canal.

Turn left here, over the canal bridge to follow Darren Road, climbing through a narrow and attractive valley. On reaching a metal gate the road becomes a grass and gravel track leading to the pass of Pegwyn-y-Bwlch. At this point you reach the Cwmcarn Scenic Drive, where a stile gives access from the Drive to Twm Barlwm. There is a fine view from here looking down into the Cwmcarn valley.

Follow a well worn track up the grassy hillside on the right leading to the hill fort on Twm Barlwm. Looking back, the Brecon Beacons can be seen on a clear day. On reaching the ditch of the Iron Age Camp, follow the rampart to the left to reach the mound (possibly a Norman motte) at the eastern end of the camp. There are very extensive views from this point.

The next part of the route can be clearly seen. A well worn track follows the crest of the ridge for several miles.

Follow this track to reach a line of electricity pylons. Then join a track which contours around the head of Blaen Brân valley, looking down on the cluster of 18th century cottages of The Square, Upper Cwmbrân.

Descend a stone track to reach a large boulder and follow a track to the left. This joins a Forestry Commission road leading down to the Mountain Air Picnic Site. On joining a tarmac road, follow it to reach the Lamb Inn. Turn right around the rear of the inn and cross a stile to the right of a ruined church. Cross a field to reach another stile and then follow a lane directly opposite, which descends to the Prince of Wales Inn. Then pass under the archway of a railway viaduct. Go past a ruined church and follow the pavement to cross the A4051 to continue along the pavement and cross the A472 to reach Pontypool Park Gates. (Cars may be left at the Leisure Centre Car Park).

The Grotto, Pontypool Park

Section II — Pontypool Park to Llanfoist (5 hours)

Start from the ornate gates of Pontypool Park (a magnificent example of wrought iron work, given to John Hanbury by his wife's friend, Sarah Churchill, Duchess of Marlborough).

Follow a path to the right of the gates and ascend between two stone walls to reach a stile. Then follow a sunken track to gain the open ridge above and the very extensive views. Go over another stile. The building behind the wall on the left is the Pontypool Park Grotto. A metal ladder in the wall gives access to the building. It was built by Lady Molly Mackworth in about 1830 and it took about seven years to complete. The materials used included limestone, quartz conglomerate, sandstone and gritstone. Of particular interest is the floor, which consists of animal teeth and pebbles arranged in various patterns. The pillars supporting the roof and the interior walls are decorated with shells of all shapes and sizes. Unfortunately the interior was badly damaged some years ago by vandals and it is now kept locked.

Return to the original route and shortly go over a stile to join a cart track. The views will now open up into the Eastern Valley. Go over another stile. Ignore a track to the right and follow the crest of the ridge looking down on the big factory of I.C.I. Go over two more stiles and shortly you will reach a raised mound with stones on the top and a small cairn erected by the Royal Air Forces Association *"in remembrance of Comrades who gave their lives during the 2nd World War"*.

At one time on this mound there stood a tall stone tower with a battlemented top. It was known as the Pontypool Folly and was built as a summer house for the Hanbury family in the 18th century. It provided a very fine viewpoint and by the 19th century it had become a well known feature in the county. In 1801, Coxe wrote: *"No traveller should quit Monmouthshire without enjoying this singular and almost boundless prospect"*.

The tower was demolished in 1939 as a security measure for it was thought that it would act as a landmark and guide enemy aircraft. In 1958 it was suggested that the tower should be reconstructed in glass, in view of the fact that Pontypool was the home of the glassmaking industry. However nothing came of this idea.

Continue along the track to reach a gate and a junction of tracks. Go straight on past a National Park sign and follow a track beside a stone wall, gradually climbing the ridge and looking down on Pontypool golf course.

Soon you descend to a dingle to pass Coed Ithel farm, over a stream and then straight on following a wide track climbing between two banks. Go through a metal gate and climb steadily to the summit of Garn Wen (trig' point) to enjoy a very fine view, weather permitting.

Now continue along the crest of the ridge with the terrain very tufty and boggy in places. Pass over Mynydd Garn-clochdy and on to cross the Blaenavon—Llanover road. Then gently ascend Mynydd-y-garn Fawr to reach the enormous pile of stones known as Carn y Defaid. From here strike across to the twin radio masts and the Foxhunter car park. This is a possible finishing point for the walk, if you have previously left a vehicle at this point.

Otherwise, follow the well defined track from the car park to the summit of the Blorenge (1,833 feet). Then make for the north east edge of the hill to obtain a bird's eye view of Abergavenny and descend the north east shoulder. Head for a stile where the track leads down to the old incline which descends steeply through the woods to reach Llanfoist wharf. Go through the tunnel under the canal and then down a lane past St Faith's church to reach Llanfoist village.

The Vale of Usk

"The Usk continued, everywhere, our amusing companion: and if, at any time, it made a more devious curve than usual, we were sure to meet it again at the next curve."

William Gilpin (1770)

Wentwood and the Vale of Usk

In Gwent the Usk Valley extends from Glangrwyne to Newport and contains beautiful river scenery, lovely stone arched bridges, fascinating churches, several castles, Roman Fort sites, ancient hill forts, picturesque churches and an early 20th century engineering marvel (Newport Transporter Bridge) and the third highest tidal rise in the world!

ROUTE 21
THE PUNCHBOWL (3 hours)

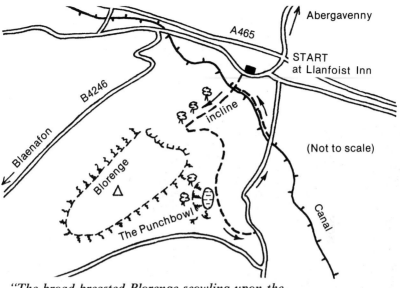

"The broad breasted Blorenge scowling upon the
plain beneath and towering magnificently and proudly."

John White (1877)

This walk explores the lower north eastern slopes of the Blorenge and provides pleasant views across Abergavenny to the surrounding hills.

Start from the Llanfoist Inn (G.R. 288134), follow the Govilon road for a short way and take the second turning on the left (F.P. sign — Blorenge 2.4km). Walk up the lane passing St Faith's Church. The name Llanfoist is derived from Llanffwyst. It is believed that Ffwyst was a saint, born in Anglesey in the 6th century, who is reputed to be the founder of this church. Crawshay Bailey, the ironmaster, is buried in the churchyard. To see his grave, go over a stone stile on the left and follow a path a short way, making for a brown marble pillar behind iron railings in the top left hand corner of the graveyard. He died on 9th January 1872 aged 82.

Follow the lane upwards beside a stream. On reaching a bend, bear right to pass through a tunnel beneath the Brecon & Abergavenny Canal. This tunnel was constructed for the old parish road to run under the canal. It is 90 yards long, 6½ ft wide and approximately 7 ft high. Above it stands the old wharf master's house. Continue to a wooden gate. On the other side, ignore a waymark to the right and keep straight on following the old Llanfoist incline through the woods where trams carrying iron from the Garnddyrys Ironworks used to travel on a double line of rails. At the bottom of the incline, by the Llanfoist Boathouse, the iron was transferred to barges and taken down to Newport.

As you climb the old incline, look out for stones with holes bored into them — they once held the tram rails in position. The first incline ends at a level platform where the winding gear was situated.

Continue upwards past a small brick hut and up the next section of incline to reach a stile. Keep climbing with a fence on the right. On emerging from the wood, head up to another stile below the great central bowl of the Blorenge north face. Look back for magnificent views of the Black Mountains, Sugar Loaf, Skirrid Fawr and eastern Gwent.

Cross the stile and turn left to follow an old tram road. Abergavenny is spread out below, with Skirrid Fawr standing proud against the sky. Follow this wide grass track around the hillside, enjoying the panoramic views. On a very clear day, to the north east, you may pick out the Clee and Malvern Hills in Shropshire and Herefordshire.

Follow the track beside a fence to a stile, then to a metal gate. Descend slightly with a fence on your left and pick up a cart track leading gently upwards to another metal gate. Go through and suddenly below you is a small lake (not marked on the Ordnance Survey map), behind it are the tree clad slopes of the 'Punch Bowl'. A good echo is possible here if the atmospheric conditions are suitable.

Cross a man-made dam along the left side of the lake and keep straight on towards a fence on the left, following a path which develops into a stony track. Climb beside a tumbling stone wall to a metal gate. Go through the gate, straight on, shortly turning left through a gap in a stone wall to descend a sunken road beneath overhanging boughs. Go over a stile and down this sunken lane, crunching through long fallen leaves, to a stile by Upper Ninfa Farm. Turn left down a tarmac road (views towards Skirrid Fawr), passing Middle and Lower Ninfa Farms. Carry on down the road to the canal. Go over a bridge and turn immediately right over a stone stile and then right under the canal bridge to follow the towpath back to Llanfoist Boathouse. Opposite this building, go right down some stone steps. Inspect the sixth step to find a memory of the old Abergavenny & Brecon Canal Company. Rejoin the original route at the bottom of the steps and return to the Llanfoist Inn.

Llanfoist Wharf, Abergavenny & Brecon Canal

ROUTE 22
THE GOOSE AND CUCKOO (2½ hours)

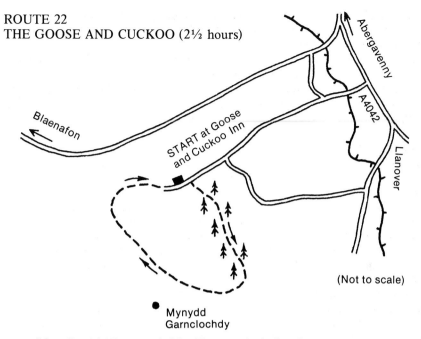

(Not to scale)

● Mynydd
Garnclochdy

*"Our list of Monmouthshire Taverns includes the
'Goose & Cuckoo', the 'Drum and Monkey', the 'Tippling
Philospher' and the 'Ramping Cat'."*

Fred J. Hando

This walk starts from an isolated inn known as "The Goose and Cuckoo" situated on the hillside west of Llanover village (G.R. 290073).

Park on a grass clearing just below the inn, by a F.P. sign (Goytre). Go through a wooden gate and follow a path through a conifer plantation and pass some lovely old beech trees with the occasional squirrel scuttling along their branches. The wide track rises gently for some distance and then descends, passing heaps of conglomerate rocks.

Through a wooden gate, turn right along a gravel track. Keep right at the next junction and follow a sunken road (a ditch between high banks). Keep right again where the track divides, following an ancient route, soon rejoining the previous track. Go right, heading up through the trees to a wooden gate. Good views can be seen from here across eastern Gwent. Notice the very fine example of stone walling on the left hand side of the gate.

Follow a track slightly to the right through a shallow gully. Keep left where it divides to join another track curving right, to reach the open hillside above. Follow a track along the north eastern side of the ridge with a stone wall on your right, past old limestone quarries. Sharp eyes will spot a lime kiln which can be examined.

The track now crosses a section of moorland which can sometimes be rather boggy. Keep just above the stone wall. An old Welsh long farm house can be seen perched on the hillside below. About quarter of a mile beyond this building, the wall bends sharply to the right.

Follow a track down between two stone walls through a wooden gate and across a track and down beside a stone wall to another gate. Keep straight on at the junction of two tracks and walk through a tunnel of trees, crunching over crispy brown leaves to yet another wooden gate. Continue along the road to the "Goose and Cuckoo" Inn.

In the 19th century Lady Llanover did much to revive and encourage Welsh literature and traditions. She was noted for keeping drunkenness out of the valley by purchasing every inn in the neighbourhood and converting them into coffee houses. The only one that escaped this fate was the "Goose and Cuckoo".

ROUTE 23
THE PILGRIMS' WAY

(3½ hours)

(Not to scale)

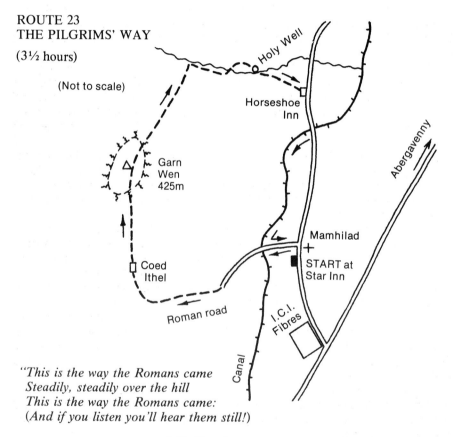

"This is the way the Romans came
Steadily, steadily over the hill
This is the way the Romans came:
(And if you listen you'll hear them still!)

A.G. Prys-Jones

76

Start from The Star Inn at Mamhilad village (to the north east of Pontypool, off A4042 at G.R. 304034). Permission must be obtained for parking your car at this inn.

Opposite the gates to Mamhilad church, turn up the road past the inn. Shortly, cross the canal and continue along the road for about half a mile, rising gently to a wide opening in the hedge on the left (by a large barn), where a good view across the surrounding countryside can be enjoyed.

Just beyond this point, on the right, a track ascends through the trees. This is the start of the Roman road. A cobbled surface winds up the hillside through a tunnel of trees. Unfortunately, parts of this ancient surface have been damaged by motorcyclists and horseriders. Historians disagree on the origin of this road, some claiming that it is merely a mediaeval packhorse route from Mamhilad to Trevethin. However, it is of interest that a Roman coin, dating from around the third century A.D. was found nearby at Troed-y-Rhiw farm. Considerable remains of this stone trackway, about half a mile in length, can be seen. At intervals, diagonal drains or gutters are evident, crossing the pavement and designed to take away surplus water.

After about ten minutes of steady climbing, you emerge into an open area. Follow the hedge on your left. On reaching the crest of the ridge, where the view ahead to the Eastern valley opens up, turn right past a Brecon Beacons National Park sign and follow a track beside a stone wall, gently climbing the ridge. Below on the left is Pontypool golf course, said to be the second highest in England and Wales.

A short descent leads to a dingle where Coed Ithel farm nestles "far from the madding crowd". Cross the farm drive and down to a stream. Keep straight on following a wide track climbing between two banks. Go through a metal gate and continue along a well defined track, climbing steadily to the summit of Garn Wen (trig' point) which provides a magnificent viewpoint.

Continue along the crest of the ridge for about a mile as far as a pronounced dip. From here, follow a track dropping to the right near the remains of a stone wall. The track soon becomes fairly steep and bends to the left to join a wide track contouring the hillside. (Tricky descent when the ferns are high). Turn left along this wide track to the top of a narrow and steep valley. To the right of a stream, a track zig zags into the valley. Lower down it passes to the right of a large beech tree. From here, a stile is soon reached. Shortly, cross the stream and follow a track down the other bank to a stile. Continuing downwards, you will come to the Holy Well. This is a small stone structure built like a fireplace with a murky pool in front of it. The Welsh name for this medieval well is Ffynnon Angaeron.

After inspecting the well, walk on to a stile and down beside the babbling stream. Soon the track broadens and passes through a wood, crossing occasional streams. A stile is reached at the edge of the wood. Continue down to a metal gate and over a stream.

Head across a field to another metal gate directly ahead. Cross the next field and through the left hand of two gates set side by side. Turn left and follow the

The Holy Well (Ffynnon Angaeron)

fence. Directly ahead you will see the Horseshoe Inn. Go down the field to a gate and up to a stile at the corner of the inn's car park.

Turn right and follow the road down to the next canal bridge. On the far side of the bridge, turn sharply left to a stile giving access to the canal. Turn left and follow the towpath under the next three bridges. On reaching the next bridge (after some distance), go through and walk up a path on the left to a stile. Turn right on to the road and follow it back to the start.

ROUTE 24
COED-Y-BWNYDD (The Wood of the Gentry)
(3½ hours)

"The encampment of Coed-y-Bunedd is formed on the summit of a commanding eminence, at the extremity of the Clytha Hills."
Archdeacon William Coxe (1801)

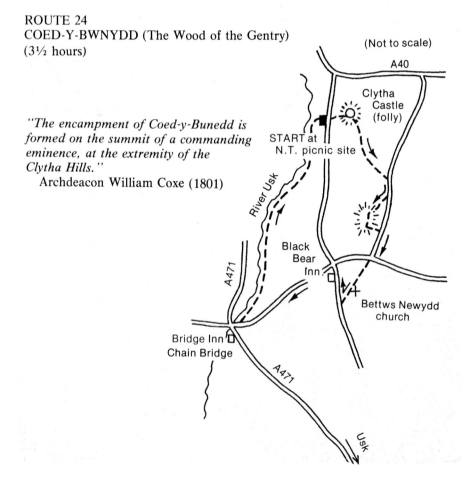

(Not to scale)

A40

Clytha Castle (folly)

START at N.T. picnic site

River Usk

A471

Black Bear Inn

Bettws Newydd church

Bridge Inn
Chain Bridge

A471

Usk

Start from the National Trust car park which is situated on the road from Bettws Newydd to Clytha, approximately half a mile south of the junction with the A40. (G.R. 362085).

Walk up to the A471 and turn left to go right through a wooden kissing gate (signposted Coed-y-Bwnydd). Head straight up past a waymark post to a wire fence. Go left along a path to reach some steps and another waymark post. Clytha Castle is now directly ahead.

The round turretted towers fool many people into thinking that a mediaeval castle stands on this hill. It is in fact a folly erected in 1790 by William Jones of Clytha House *"for the purpose of relieving a mind sincerely afflicted by the love of a most excellent wife"*. These words are part of an inscription affixed to the outside of the building.

The "Castle" has been restored by the Landmark Trust, who specialise in doing up follies and unusual buildings. It is now let as self-catering accommodation for holiday-makers.

It has been suggested that this Gothic style castle was designed by the architect Nash who was doing other work in this area in 1790.

Go across the field to a stile and over a simple footbridge. Keep straight on across the driveway, following a wide path through the trees to a stile at the end of the wood. Go straight across this field to a marker post. Follow a fence to the left and go through a gap in the corner of the field. Turn left and immediately right. Follow a hedge on the right to the corner of a field, then turn left, keeping the hedge on your right, to a stile. Keep straight on over two stiles until you reach a

Clytha Castle   *19th century engraving*

road. Turn right and follow the road for some distance. Keep straight on at junction. After a few hundred yards, go over a stile on the right. Cross a field to the right of a barn to a ladder stile and a National Trust sign indicating that this is Coed-y-Bwnydd.

Go straight on passing through two fortification ditches to reach the hill fort plateau.

Archdeacon Coxe came here in 1798 and wrote:-

> *"The western side overhangs the meandering Usk*
> *and commands a beautiful view of the northern parts*
> *of the county which will amply repay the traveller*
> *for the trouble of ascending the summit."*

A good time to come here is in the bluebell season, for they grow in abundance on the summit of this hill fort.

Keep straight on following the track (and descend) into a ditch on the south western side. Follow a path in the ditch around to the left, then out of the ditch and around to reach a National Trust sign and kissing gate on the eastern side of the fort.

Turn right and follow the road downhill, enjoying the view. Go left at a junction and in six yards turn right over a stile (signposted Bettws Newydd church 0.6 km). Go straight on across the field to a stile; over, and follow a hedge on your left down to a stile. Cross and go straight across the field to a stile to the right of a house. Follow a hedge on your right and go down to a metalled road to find a stile in the wall on the left, giving access to a churchyard.

Bettws Newydd is one of the finest little churches in Gwent. The correct spelling is Betws. It means an oratory, or a place of prayer, and was founded by Aeddon who also built churches at Clytha (now in ruins) and at Bryngwyn, near Raglan.

Carved Rood Screen at Bettws Newydd Church

This church was renamed Bettws Newydd (i.e. the New Oratory) because it was largely reconstructed at the end of the 15th century. The beautiful rood screen and rood loft were erected near the end of the 15th century. In Gwent, only two other such lofts exist and these can be found at Llangwm and Redwick.

Go through a kissing gate at the church entrance and turn left down the road and right at the next junction to follow the road to the Black Bear Inn. Turn left. Above, to the right, is a tree-covered mound which may have been the site of a Norman motte and bailey castle.

Follow this road for about three quarters of a mile into the Usk Valley to a F.P. sign on the right (Clytha Park 4 km). Go over a stile and follow a path through a wood to a stile. (This is a section of the Usk Valley Walk). Continue through a field between a wood and the river, first to a wooden gate, then to a metal gate, and pass below Brynderwen farm (a fine, solid looking building). Continue to a stile, then to a fence and up to a metal gate by a telegraph pole. Go through the gate and left to a stile, then a metal gate, and keep left past a barn to follow a gravel track. Go over a stile on the left to follow the top of a steep bank above the river. Follow a hedge on the left to a stile. Cross over and descend to a stile by the riverside and follow the river bank to a gate and a stile. Turn right and follow the track back to the starting point and car park.

ROUTE 25
KEMEYS COMMANDER
(1½ hours)

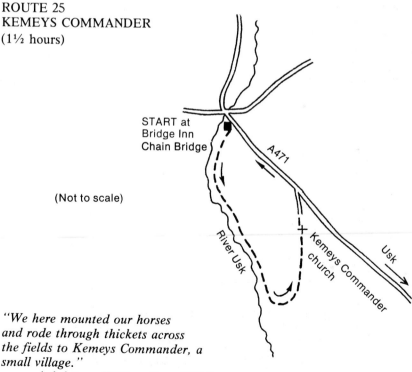

(Not to scale)

"We here mounted our horses and rode through thickets across the fields to Kemeys Commander, a small village."
Achdeacon William Coxe (1801)

Start from the Bridge Inn at Chain Bridge on the A471 about five miles from Usk (G.R. 346055).

The first bridge over the Usk at this point was washed away by a flood in 1690 and money was raised to build a new one. This was erected in 1730, built of solid oak, and was known as Pont Kemeys. In 1829, this bridge was replaced with one built by Brown Lennox of Pontypridd. Being supported by sturdy chains, it became known as Chain Bridge. However, it was demolished in 1906 when the present one was built by a contractor from Neath (George Palmer). No chains were used in the construction this time, but the bridge retained its name.

Chain Bridge, Vale of Usk

From the car park walk to the river bank and follow the riverside footpath to the left. This path follows the river bank for about a mile through a very pleasant section of the Usk Valley. On the opposite bank of the river is the route of the Usk Valley Walk and the wooded slopes of Graig-y-Pandy.

After passing a strip of woodland on the left and crossing three stiles, follow a fence on the left and shortly go right through a metal gate to join a track leading past Lower House Farm. A tarmac road now leads to Kemeys Commander church which is 15th century and has a fine timber porch. The name of this church is said to be derived from Edward Kemeys, commander of the army under Dru de Balodun at the conquest of Upper Gwent, or perhaps it was a commandery of the Knights Templars to whom the patronage of the church belonged. It is one of the smallest churches in Gwent and contains the remnants of a rood screen and has a stone altar, which is now a rare sight in Wales. There is a tiny window one foot square in the south wall which seems to serve no real purpose.

From the church follow the road to reach the A471. Turn left and walk *with care* back to the starting point.

ROUTE 26
ST MARY'S CHURCH (1½ hours)

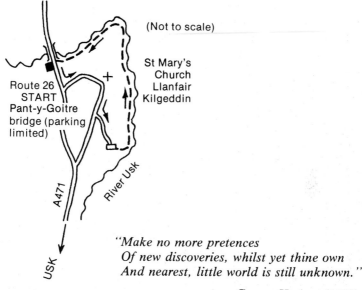

(Not to scale)

St Mary's
Church
Llanfair
Kilgeddin

Route 26
START
Pant-y-Goitre
bridge (parking
limited)

A471

River Usk

USK

"Make no more pretences
Of new discoveries, whilst yet thine own
And nearest, little world is still unknown."

George Herbert (1633)

Start from Pant-y-Goitre bridge (G.R. 348088), which is situated on the A471 new Llanvihangel Gobion.

Follow the A471 south to turn left shortly along a lane which leads to the little church of St Mary's at Llanfair Kilgeddin. (Alternative starting point).

Notice the interesting cross in the churchyard which depicts Mary and Child on one side and the Crucifixion on the other. Unfortunately the church is generally kept locked, but this is probably necessary to protect the unusual wall pictures inside. They were carried out by Heywood Sumner in 1880 using a sgraffito technique (cut away plaster) to illustrate local scenes and the Benedicite. The church itself is not particularly interesting and was largely rebuilt in 1876.

Outside the churchyard gate, turn left along the tarmac road and walk gently up hill. Just past a cottage on the right, turn left down a lane. Keep right at a metal gate and follow the lane for some distance, passing farm buildings to a metal gate.

Go straight across a field to the river bank. Turn left and walk beside the Usk. Go over a stile and through a small copse. Then over a stile by a fisherman's hut and along the grass bank beside an attractive section of river. (N.B. The Usk Valley Walk is on the other side of the river).

Wall painting at St Mary's Church, Llanfair Kilgeddin

Pant-y-Goitre Bridge

Cross a small footbridge and a stile. To your left can be seen St Mary's Church and the Sugar Loaf mountain behind. Cross a stream and a stile and continue through the next field, passing Weaver's Pool on the right. (Good views towards the Sugar Loaf and Skirrid Fawr). On the opposite bank of the Usk can be seen the National Trust picnic site and riverside walk at Clytha.

Go over a small ladder stile and follow a bend in the river to walk beside a fence with the Usk now flowing from the west. Over a neat wooden ladder stile on the right, go past a fisherman's hut and climb a concrete slipway to a stile. Continue along the river bank to a metal gate and cross the next field to a gate near the elegant Pant-y-Goitre bridge and your starting point.

> *"Travels at home are cheap and safe. Salvation comes mounted on the wings of meditation. He that doth live at home, and learns to know God and himself, needeth no no further to go."*
>
> George Herbert (1633)

ROUTE 27 (See page 86 for Map)
USK VALLEY WALK (9 hours)

> *"We passed... under deep Wentwood,*
> *above the solemn curves and esses of the river."*
>
> Arthur Machen (1920)

The river Usk is the principal river of Gwent (the Wye is half English) and flows through the centre of the county. It rises on the Carmarthen Fan in Dyfed and after a course of some forty miles it enters the county through a pass near Llanwenarth, flowing below the mountains of Mynydd Pen-y-Fal and Blorenge to pass Abergavenny. From here it meanders down to Usk and past the Wentwood escarpment to Caerleon. From there, it flows muddily down to the Bristol Channel at Newport.

On its journey through the heart of Gwent, the Usk is joined by many other smaller rivers such as the Gwenffrwyd, Gavenny, Berthin, Olwy, Sôr, Afon Llwyd and Ebbw Fach.

This route is waymarked throughout its length and starts from the Ship Inn (G.R. 342903) on the south side of the Usk in Old Caerleon. To follow the route, just look for the yellow arrows with yellow dots which will lead you northwards through the Vale of Usk to Abergavenny. The route may be walked in either direction. Strip Maps are available from the Public Relations Officer, Gwent County Council, County Hall, Cwmbrân, Gwent.

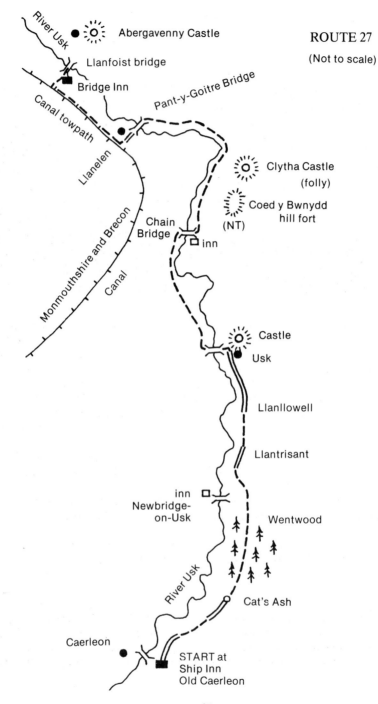

River Usk

Abergavenny Castle

ROUTE 27

(Not to scale)

Llanfoist bridge

Bridge Inn

Pant-y-Goitre Bridge

Canal towpath

Clytha Castle

(folly)

Llanelen

Coed y Bwnydd hill fort

(NT)

Chain Bridge

inn

Monmouthshire and Brecon

Canal

Castle

Usk

Llanllowell

Llantrisant

inn

Newbridge-on-Usk

Wentwood

River Usk

Cat's Ash

Caerleon

START at
Ship Inn
Old Caerleon

Glen Usk

After walking through Old Caerleon, a Roman route is soon followed over Chepstow Hill, with fine views over the Usk Valley leading on by road to Cat's Ash. This hamlet takes its name from the sign of an inn of that name that once stood here. Its sign depicted a cat sitting on the branch of an ash tree.

Above Cat's Ash the route follows a forest track on the western side of the Wentwood escarpment, which provides a magnificent view of the Usk Valley and to the north of the county. The white Mansion that is beautifully situated on the other side of the river is a late Georgian house built in 1820, near the site of an early ironworks, for Sir Digby Mackworth.

Descend past the ruins of Bertholey House which was once a seat of the Kemeys family. It was destroyed by fire in 1905 and, in a field below the house, are the remains of a small chapel.

Near here is Newbridge-on-Usk where a fine stone bridge spans the river, built by the same man who constructed the famous bridge of Pontypridd.

A road section now takes you to Llantrisant village where perhaps a welcome pause will be made for refreshment at the Royal Oak Inn.

From Llantrisant follow a footpath to the hamlet of Llanllowell where the road is followed to Usk Bridge.
Bridge.

Cross the bridge to the west bank of the river and follow a riverside path past the Island picnic site. Soon after, you will pass the Prioress Mill at Rhadyr, which was still in operation until a few years ago. It was built in the 16th century for grinding corn and obtained its power from the Berthin Brook, a tributary of the Usk.

The path climbs above the river to pass Estavarney where the remains of an ancient Iron Age Camp may be seen. It is also the site of an ironworks established by monks.

On the other side of the river can be seen the derelict windmill of Llancayo, which is a well-known landmark in the Usk Valley.

Walk down to the river again to reach Chain Bridge. Cross the river and follow the Bettws Newydd road for a short way. Over a stile on the left, follow a path through the trees, down to the riverside to pass the imposing Brynderwen farm.

Further on, down by the river can be seen the remains of Trostrey forge. Coxe came here in 1801 when the forge was still in operation and the iron bar was sent via *"Tredonnoc bridge and then by the Usk to Newport and Bristol"*.

Soon the National Trust riverside walk at Clytha is reached, below the castellated towers of Clytha Castle which can be seen peeping through the trees (a folly built in 1790 by William Jones of Clytha House in memory of his wife — see Route 24).

Continue by footpath and lane to reach Pant-y-Goitre bridge and follow a riverside path past the village of Bryn. Then, continuing beside the river to pass a rickety wooden suspension bridge (no right of way), known locally as "Mr Pym's Bridge". It was built for Mr Leslie Pym, a one-time M.P. On the other side of the river can be seen the Boat House which is used by fishermen and, behind it, the tower of Llanover Church.

After another mile, the site of Castell Arnoult is passed, where a shallow mound is all that remains of the fortified home of the Welsh Chieftain, Sietsylt. He was murdered with his followers at a banquet held at Abergavenny Castle on Christmas Day in 1177 by the notorious Baron William de Braose.

The riverside path then leads to the three arched stone bridge of Llanelen which was built in 1821 by John Upton of Gloucester.

Llanelen Church has a remarkable sundial which can be seen in the nave. It was previously mounted in the churchyard wall and resembles the bowl of a font. A granite tombstone has been laid in memory of Sir Thomas Phillips who was Mayor of Newport at the time of the Chartist riots in 1839. He was injured while reading the Riot Act and his bravery was awarded with a knighthood.

The village once had two pubs, the Hanbury Arms and the Red Lion. But the thirsty walker will be disappointed for they were purchased in the 19th century by Lady Llanover, who closed one and turned the other into a temperance inn with the sign of Y Seren Gobaith (The Star of Hope), but this inn has since disappeared as well.

From Llanelen follow the waymarked route through the village and up to the canal towpath which is now followed, with very fine views across Abergavenny to Skirrid Fawr, to reach Llanfoist Wharf and boathouse. From here, descend some stone steps, cross a stile and follow the lane down past Llanfoist church to cross the B4246. Now follow a lane which soon takes you underneath the Heads of the Valleys road and then down to Llanfoist bridge where, if the time is right, a well earned drink and snack may be obtained at the Bridge Inn.

Wentwood Area

"My vagrant heart goes stealing on such a day as this,
Through haunted paths of Wentwood, all shadowy and still,
Where Usk is gently sighing 'neath the flooding tides' full kiss,
And little tracks are tangled 'midst the trees on Kemeys hill."

Myfanwy Haycock

The Foresters' Oaks, Wentwood

This area can be defined as the country bounded on the west by the A449, the B4235 to the north and east and the M4 to the south. It contains the once Royal Chase of Wentwood Forest, the Agrarian Castles, the beautiful Cwm and Mounton Valleys, the twin hills of Mynydd Alltir Fach and Gray Hill, prehistoric stone circles, standing stones, hill forts and some fascinating churches.

At one time the Royal Forest of Wentwood had its own forest laws and courts were held twice a year at Forester's Oaks. Sheep stealing was regarded as a serious offence and culprits were usually hung on one of the oak trees. The last offender was dealt with in this manner in 1829.

Much of the original forest disappeared in the 17th and 18th centuries when considerable felling took place in order to provide oak for building ships of war. This heavy demand for timber continued during the two World Wars in the 20th century.

WAYMARKED WALKS

Six waymarked walks have been set up by Gwent County Council in conjunction with the Forestry Commission. They all start from picnic sites and are waymarked by a system of coloured arrows so that people may explore these woods without fear of losing their way.

The routes are all circular and are described in a leaflet published by Gwent County Council (see address on page 141).

ROUTE 28
CIRCUIT OF WENTWOOD (6½ hours)

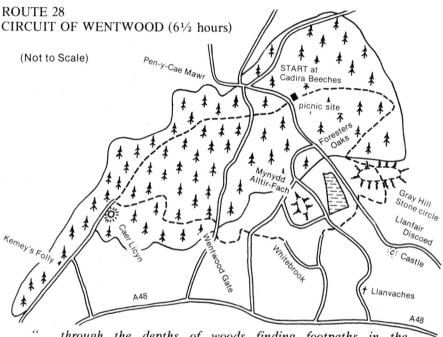

"... through the depths of woods finding footpaths in the most unsuspected places that we had never dreamed of."

Arthur Machen (1918)

Start from the Cadira Beeches picnic site on the Pen-y-cae Mawr to Llanfair Discoed road, near its highest point (G.R. 422948).

From the picnic site turn left and follow a forest road in a north easterly direction. Ignore a junction to the left and carry on to reach the junction of five paths in a large clearing. Keep straight on, soon steadily going downhill to reach a T-junction. Turn right and descend on a broad forest road. At the next junction turn right along a forest road which is followed for about a mile, ignoring side turnings to ascend to a T-junction by a gate. Turn left and shortly keep right beside a hedge to bear left, following a path up Gray Hill.

Soon you are looking down on Wentwood Reservoir and across to the highest point of the forest near Wentwood Lodge where the tallest tree can be seen. This is a Wellingtonia which is more usually seen growing in Sierra Nevada in Canada.

Keep left beside a fence, following a well worn path and up the final slope to reach the summit. Follow the path to the left along the crest of the ridge. Notice the outcrops of conglomerate rock which is sometimes referred to as pudding stone.

Turn right at a track junction by a waymark post (pointing the other way) and keep left at the next junction, which leads you down to a prehistoric stone circle at an altitude of about 900 ft. It is 32 ft in diameter and may have once surrounded a large cairn of stones or a barrow. The circle dates back to the Bronze Age and is some 4,000 years old at a rough guess.

By the obvious standing stone, turn right to follow a track in a south easterly direction. Ahead can be seen the Coastal Plain and the Severn Estuary.

On reaching a broad cart track on the lower slopes of the hill, go right to soon pass below a small cottage and then another cottage on the left. Climb a rise and look out for a little path on the left giving access to a metal stile. Follow a hedge on the left down (notice old sunken lane in the hedge) to reach a metal gate and the road.

Turn left along road and almost immediately go through a metal gate on the far side of a cottage. Pass the front of the cottage and through a farmyard (Right of Way) and cross a field to reach another metal gate.

Keep hedge on right to reach a stile from which the track goes on to reach a metal fence and curves around to reach a stile and F.P. sign. Go left to the road and turn right. After about 100 yards go left at a F.P. sign (Llanvaches 1 km). Cross a stile and the path heads up through a pleasant copse to reach another stile. Notice an old quarry concealed in the undergrowth on the left. Go over the stile and turn left along a road which is followed down to a junction. Turn right (signposted Whitebrook) and go uphill to Plas Talgarth, where you will see a "stone toadstool" and a barn with a dovecote in its upper part.

Carry on along this road, with pleasant views, to pass Whitebrook Cottage. On reaching Trout Farm go left through a metal gate (Do not be put off by sign referring to trout sales — this is a Right of Way). Follow the drive down to trout farm. Go through a gate and turn right around the back of a building, past a barn and through another gate. Cross a field, through a gate to cross the next field and through another gate. Then bear diagonally left towards a telegraph pole to find a stile in the hedge. Now follow a line of electricity poles and a fence to reach a stile in the hedge (just below a house). Turn left on road to reach a junction. Follow the road to the right and after about 200 yards go right by a F.P. sign (Wentwood 0.6 km). Then over a stile and turn left following a broad track leading up through a wood. Bear right at a track junction at the summit of this wooded hill, to descend to a stile and F.P. sign (Arcade Road 0.4 km). Turn right on road, enjoying views across to Mynydd Alltir Fach. Pass a cottage on the left and soon you will reach a Forestry Commission track on the left (Riding Trail sign).

Go through a metal gate and after about 100 yards turn left at a track junction, bearing right soon at the next junction. This pleasant path contours around the lower slopes of Wentwood in an area known as Wentwood Gate. Descend to a track junction and keep right. Ignore other tracks from the right and keep straight on to cross a stream and then go through a metal gate to reach a broad track.

Turn right and follow the broad track up hill to ascend a forest road. After a big bend in a clearing, where views have opened out across Wentwood, take a wide track on the left, back into the woods again and heading in a north westerly direction, ascending to emerge on the crest of the ridge by a cottage. Go right along a grass track, taking the main path on the left at the next junction. It is overhung by trees and is the old Roman route from Chepstow to Caerleon.

Before long the grass track joins a forest road. After about quarter of a mile leave the forest road and follow the continuation of the old track up through the trees in the footsteps of the Romans. Ignore all tracks to the right. Further on, the track follows the edge of the Wentwood northern escarpment. However the trees obscure the fine view that would otherwise be seen across the Vale of Usk.

Passing through a wooden gate you bear right soon and follow the path uphill. It becomes a wide track between Christmas trees and leads up to a road. Go straight across and follow a forest road to reach Wentwood Lodge picnic site and some ancient tumuli. Continue along the forest road past an ariel and in due course you will reach the Pen y cae mawr to Llanfair Discoed road and your starting point at Cadira Beeches.

This walk is not advisable in the height of summer when flies can be very unpleasant. Some sections of the route can also be wet and muddy (particularly after heavy rain), and wellingtons are not advisable for such a long walk.

ROUTE 29
THE COOMBE VALLEY (3 hours)

> *"The Coombe was ever dark, ancient and dark*
> *Its mouth is stopped with bramble, thorn and brier."*
>   Edward Thomas

Start from the King's Arms Inn at Llanfair Discoed (G.R. 447924).

Follow the road past the side of the inn (opposite the school). After a few hundred yards turn right over a stile (F.P. sign — Earlswood 2 km) and head straight up a field to reach a stile. Cross a drive and keep straight on to shortly recross the drive. Go over a stile and walk beside a hedge to reach a stile in the corner of the field. Over the stile and turn half right to cross another stile. Follow the hedge on the right to reach a metal gate.

Turn left along a rough track which provides good views across the Coombe Valley to Earlswood Common and Lower Argoed. Go through a metal gate and the track contours around a beautiful landscape to pass a ruined house. Pass

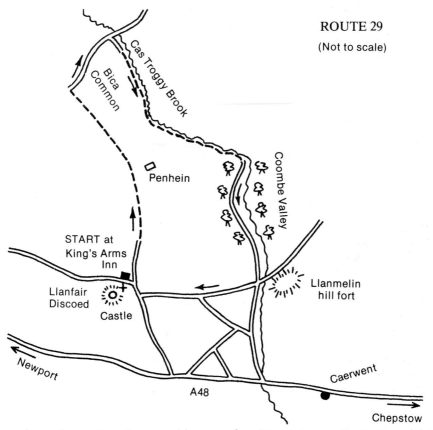

through another gate and on reaching a surfaced track by a cottage, turn right and descend into the valley, crossing Bica Common.

Having descended almost to the floor of the valley, follow a gravel track to the right. Go through a metal gate and then just before reaching another gate and cottages, turn left by an oak tree to follow a path directly down to a stream. Turn right and follow a path through the valley close to the stream to reach a stone stile. Over this, and another stile in a fence, to carry on through a field beside a hedge above the stream. Then through a gate and on beside a fence to another gate and then on to reach a footpath sign and a gate.

Turn right along a rough track which soon crosses a stone bridge. Now follow a tarmac road through this beautiful valley. The remains of Upper Coombe Mill are passed on the right and, further down the valley, is a rambling house called The Coombe where the stream has been tamed to flow through the ornamental gardens and then descend with a flourish via two small cascades. Beyond this point the valley starts to broaden.

Ahead can be seen a tree covered hill which is the site of Llanmelin Iron Age hill fort, which was once occupied by the Silures.

Turn right at the road junction and follow the road back to Llanfair Discoed village.

The village has several items of interest which may be observed at the end of this walk. Look out for a squat tower with square holes in its sides. This was once used as a dovecote. It looks completely out of place in its present situation, wedged between a house and a garage and most people pass it by without a second glance.

Across the road is an old farmhouse with the date 1635 and a Welsh inscription carved on a stone over its whitewashed porch.

The church has been much restored and rebuilt. Of particular interest is a stone set into the wall of the porch. At one time it used to be the churchyard stile, but no doubt because it was considered worthwhile to preserve the following rhyme, it was removed to its present position.

"Who ever hear on Sunday,
Will practis playing at ball
It may be before Monday
The Devil will have you all."

Anon

Coombe Valley

This inscription is said to be the work of a stone mason who may have listened to the fearful sermons of William Wroth of Llanvaches, a neighbouring village.

Hidden in a tangle of trees above the churchyard are the ruins of a 13th century castle (situated in the grounds of a private bungalow). The ruins consist of a shell of two round towers perched on the edge of a small encampment, the fragments of a curtain wall and some miscellaneous heaps of masonry said to represent the keep. Apparently the castle was originally of considerable size.

94

The Coastal Plain

The Coastal Path at Goldcliff

"As far westward as the eye can reach, the plains run away, penned between Wentwood and the Severn and intersected by inumerate stagnant ditches, the Gwentland folk call 'rhines'."

E. Elliot Stock
"The Land of the Lords Marchers"

Gwent unfortunately lacks a scenic coastline with a sandy beach. However, the southern edge of the county contains many interesting features and the views across the muddy Severn Estuary can often be very attractive, particularly in the right lighting conditions. It is also an area of special interest to bird watchers and is rated very highly as a location for observing wading birds.

This area of land was reclaimed from the sea by the Romans in the Third Century. It is criss-crossed by an intricate system of reens that drain the land and provide a picturesque scene, with "mint sauce" water lined by willow trees.

The coastal plain is divided into two parts by the mouth of the Usk. Between the Usk and the Wye is the area known as the Caldicot Level and that between the Usk and the Rhymney is referred to as the Wentllwg Level (or more correctly Gwynllwg Level). Locally they are known as "the moors" and they contain some of the deepest and richest soil in the county. At one time the reens were crossed by local people with the aid of jumping poles or "powt".

The walker will discover that this is a land of legends, castles, churches bearing memories of a great flood, a huge steel works, a Bishop's Palace, ancient manor houses, farms, sites of priories, a salmon fishery of Roman origin, an ancient ferry crossing, the longest railway tunnel in Britain and views of the second longest road bridge and the highest tidal rise in Britain.

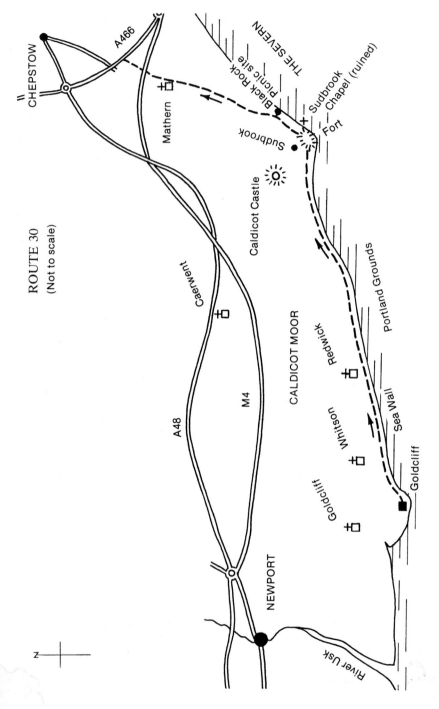

ROUTE 30
(Not to scale)

CHEPSTOW

A466

Mathern

THE SEVERN

Black Rock Picnic site

Sudbrook Chapel (ruined)

Fort

Sudbrook

Caldicot Castle

Caerwent

A48

M4

CALDICOT MOOR

Portland Grounds

Redwick

Sea Wall

Whitson

Goldcliff

Goldcliff

NEWPORT

River Usk

N

ROUTE 30
THE COASTAL FOOTPATH (7 hours)

> *"There twice a day the Severn fills,*
> *The salt water rushes by*
> *And hushes half the babbling Wye*
> *And makes a silence in the hills."*

A.L. Tennyson

Waymarked for its entire length between Goldcliff and the outskirts of Chepstow this route does not require detailed description. On this walk you will pass many locations of historical and natural interest and these are listed in order of appearance.

Start at the sea wall at Goldcliff (G.R. 374823).

> *"Goldcliff, singularly famous for its transparent shining*
> *rocks and cliffs, and the gilded sands that lie about it."*
> Nathan Rogers (Early 18th century)

According to the 12th century writer Giraldus Cambrensis the name of these cliffs refers to the golden appearance of the rock when the sun reflects on them. It would seem that the bands of sandstone contained particles of yellow mica which must have made quite a sparkling effect. However, these cliffs are now smothered by the limestone blocks of the present day sea defences, so unfortunately we can no longer enjoy the spectacle.

On the headland to the west is the site of Goldcliff Priory (on private land). Founded in 1113 by the Norman, Robert de Chandos, as a Benedictine establishment, it was occupied by a prior and twelve monks. Over the years the priory was eroded by the sea and eventually collapsed. Some earthworks near the lighthouse on top of the cliff are believed to be the foundations of some of the outhouses attached to the priory.

Near here is the site of the Goldcliff salmon fishery. Timber racks stretch out along the foreshore holding rows of aluminium baskets 5 to 6 ft in length and tapering from 2 ft in diameter at the mouth to 6 inches at the tail and known as "putchers". Originally they were made from withy cut from a six acre plantation at Llanwern.

The putchers are set up at the start of the season in May and left in place until August. When the unsuspecting salmon swim blearily through the murky Severn Estuary, they find themselves in the baskets when the ebbing tide leaves them high and dry. This form of fishing has been carried out here for many centuries and may even date back to Roman times.

Having explored the history of the starting point, the route continues along the top of the sea wall towards Chepstow.

The sea wall was originally constructed by the Romans for a total distance of twenty miles between Sudbrook and Rhymney, possibly for the purpose of growing wheat on this large area of reclaimed land. In 1878 an inscribed stone of Roman origin was discovered below the sea wall near Goldcliff stating (in Latin) that *"a century of the 1st cohort built 33½paces"*. This stone can now be seen in Caerleon museum.

Over the centuries these extensive sea defences have been re-shaped and improved and today there is a massive stone embankment. Henry III even set up a Court of Sewers to look after the drainage of this area and Dutchmen were employed in the 17th century to strengthen the sea wall.

About two miles from Goldcliff is a sinister looking building known as Porton House which is reputed to have been a base for smugglers at one time. Behind this house is a small cottage with a huge salmon painted on one wall — obviously associated with another fisherman's tale!

From Porton House a short detour can be made by following a footpath inland to visit Whitson Church which has a leaning tower counterbalanced by a curious stone "thimble". An inscription inside the church, about 5 ft above the ground, records the height reached by the waters of the Great Flood of 1606. A high tide overwhelmed the earthen banks and flooded the entire moorland between Cardiff and Portskewett. Twenty eight parishes were inundated over an area 24 miles long by 4 miles wide and some 2,000 people were drowned.

Inscription in porch of Redwick Church

An extract from a pamphlet written at that time records the incident as follows :-

> *"The number of men drowned are not known to exceed*
> *2,000 and all the wild beasts and vermin tried to*
> *escape from the water by getting to the most elevated*
> *banks and parts of the land, where were collected dogs,*
> *cats, mice in abundance and strange to say that none of*
> *them offered to annoy the other, but in a gentle sort of way*
> *freely enjoyed the liberty of life."*

Most of the churches on these moors display a plaque commemorating this tragic day in 1606.

Beyond Porton House, three large pipelines reach out to the estuary carrying waste material from the Llanwern Steel Works.

Soon the tower of Redwick Church comes into sight (see Route 33 for further details about this village).

Further on, Cold Harbour Pill comes into view; a small inlet which was once the site of the town and harbour of Abergwaetha, destroyed by erosion. Chapel tump marks the site of a chapel that was once used by this port.

Between Coldharbour Pill and Magor Pill can be seen the remains of a prehistoric forest, established on a peat bed.

Bird life is very evident in this area. Huge flocks of Dunlin may be seen and large numbers of Gulls, Curlews and Shelducks.

South east of Rogiet the path crosses a firing range used for practice by Army and Police rifle clubs. If a red flag is flying, you may have to wait a short time before an official will let you proceed.

At Caldicot Pill, a footpath gives access to a pub if you are in need of refreshment at this stage of the walk.

Further on along the coast are the remains of an Iron Age Camp at Sudbrook. This massive earthwork enclosure has been eroded on one side by the Severn cutting into the rocks at the base of the cliff. It is possible that the Romans made use of this site when they first landed in Gwent. They built and maintained roads connecting it with their later fort at Caerwent. Bricks, Coins and other Roman remains have been found here.

In the 13th century, a Norman church was erected inside the enclosure. It has been in ruins for about two centuries and the last burial which took place within its walls was that of Mr Blethin Smith, who had been master of a merchant vessel and the owner of a small estate at this place. His will, dated 1755, requested that his body *"should be buried in the eastern end of the Chancel of the decayed Church of Sudbrook, as near the wall as may be, attended by six sea faring men as bearers".*

Leaving the coast, go down a path between a cottage and the wall of the Severn Tunnel Pumping Station and into Sudbrook village.

This small village was built when the Severn Tunnel was being constructed to house the workers and provide them with a school, hospital, mission hall, infirmary and a coffee tavern (no pub!). The man responsible for all this work was Thomas Walker, who commenced the Severn Tunnel scheme in 1880.

During construction, unexpected problems were encountered, with difficult rock, sand and clay to tunnel through. In 1883 the workings were flooded by an enormous underground spring (later christened 'The Great Spring'). To deal with this problem, Walker built the pumping station and used Cornish Beam Engines to lower the level of water in the tunnel. 24 million gallons of water are removed in an average day. In one year this amount of water would form a lake of 1,000 acres in extent and 10 yards deep.

The 4-mile tunnel was completed in 1886 and the first passenger train passed through it on December 1st of that year.

Sudbrook Church

From Sudbrook village the waymarks lead you along a lane to reach Blackrock where there is a picnic area. This is the site of the so called "New Passage" which dates back to ancient times. It is believed to be the spot where Julius Frontinus and his Romans first landed on their invasion of Siluria. At that time the Charston Rock, or Black Rock as it was then called, was part of the mainland, but it now lies some distance out in the Channel with a light standing on it.

A tale may be told here of Charles I, who was fleeing south from Cromwell's men. He was only a couple of hours ahead of his pursuers when he reached Black Rock. The king was taken safely across the Severn, but when the boatmen returned, they found the pursuing Roundheads waiting for them. Forced at the point of a sword to take the furious Ironside soldiers into their craft, the ferrymen started back across the river. But the soldiers never reached the English coast alive. On some pretext the Royalist oarsmen persuaded them to leave their boats on the rocky reef known as English Stones. It was low tide at the time, but when the swift tide started up the channel the boats had gone and the king's pursuers were swept away.

Cromwell was furious and banned the ferry which was not used again for nearly a century. It then became known as the New Passage.

A regular public ferry service was introduced in the 18th century and in 1863 it passed into the ownership of the Bristol and South Wales Union Company, who erected hotels on both sides of the Severn to provide accommodation for the passengers. The Great Western Railway Company took over the service in 1868 which they worked with paddle steamers.

Today, all that remains is the stone jetty, a few iron rings and an overgrown railway cutting where the passenger trains once passed. There used to be a long wooden jetty jutting out into the estuary, where passengers embarked and boarded the iron steamer which sailed across the Severn to the New Passage Inn on the Gloucestershire side.

However, the opening of the Severn tunnel and the rival ferry service at Beachley to Aust reduced trade. When the pier burnt down, the service was finally closed.

The Severn Estuary is one of Britain's biggest estuaries and is under constant pressure for industrial development with new factories, nuclear power stations, a possible airport and the mammoth Severn Barrage scheme. It is, at the same time, an area of great historical and natural interest with a large wildlife population.

In the centre of the estuary can be seen Denny Island, which provides a tiny breeding ground for Herring and Black Headed Gulls. About 100 years ago a fox was killed on this island. It must have taken advantage of low water at Spring tide to make a visit there.

It has been calculated that some ten million tons of mud are stirred up by swirling currents and tidal action which accounts for the murky colour.

From Blackrock the waymarked path takes the walker away from the coast and across the Caldicot Level to Mathern village.

To the west can be seen the chimneys of St Pierre which takes its name from a Norman owner, and the land surrounding it is now the site of a well known golf course.

Nearby is Moynes Court, a Jacobean mansion which has retained a 14th century gatehouse of a former manor house.

St Theodric's Church, Mathern

The final point of interest on the walk is Mathern village, which has a fascinating history. The church of St Theodric is a fine structure consisting of a nave with north and south aisles, chancel, south porch, and a lofty square embattled tower. On one side of the tower is a massive sundial.

Mathern is said to have derived its name from Merthyr Tewdric (the Martyrdom of Theodric) who was buried here in the 7th century. An inscription relating the story of Tewdric can be seen inside the church on the north wall of the chancel.

> "Here lyeth intombed the body of Theodrick, king of
> Morganrick or Glamorgan, commonly called St Tewdrick
> and accounted a martyr because he was slain in a battle
> against the Saxons, being then pagans, and in defence of
> the Christian Religion. The battle was fought at Tintern
> where he obtained a great victory. He died on his way
> homeward, three days after the battle, having taken order
> with Marvice his son, who succeeded him in his Kingdom
> that in the same place he should happen to decease, a
> church should be built and his body buried in ye same place,
> which was accordingly performed in the year 600."

Adjacent to the church is Mathern Palace, which was the residence of the Bishops of Llandaff from the 15th to the 18th centuries. It then fell into decay to be later restored by H. Avary Tipping in 1894. It is still a private house.

There is a strange story that when a wall of the Palace was being dismantled, the skeleton of a man was found with a drinking cup beside him, walled up in a recess. On exposure to the air the remains fell to dust.

Another item of interest in the village is St Tewdric's Well, where it is reputed that the dying man's wounds were washed at this spot. He was being taken on a cart drawn by two stags towards the Severn Estuary. When the cart stopped, a spring started to flow from the ground. His followers had intended to bury him on the island of Flat Holm, but he died here at Mathern and that was where he was buried.

The well is certainly very old, for it was mentioned by Nennius in his "Historia Britorium" which he wrote in the 8th century. Unfortunately the well was recently renovated and given a modern look.

From Mathern the route crosses the M4 and passes through fields to the A466 where roads may be followed into Chepstow.

From there, one may proceed to Monmouth either by way of the Wye Valley Walk or along Offa's Dyke Path.

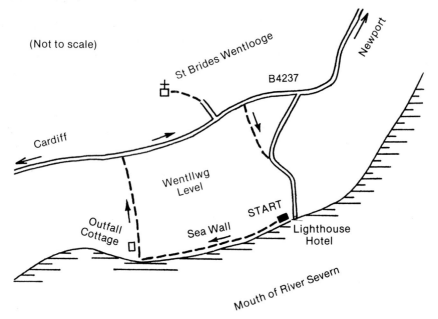

"The soile by south towards Severn is sumwhat low
and fulle of dikes to drain it."

John Leland (16th century)

Start from the Lighthouse Hotel (large car park G.R. 300816).

On the seaward side of the car park go over a stile and up some steps. Turn right along a track following the foreshore. An old pillbox — a gun post of World War II vintage — is passed on the right.

This is unfortunately a dismal and chaotic shoreline. However, even the murky waters of the Severn can be beautiful in the right lighting conditions. Huge limestone blocks now form the sea defences which originally consisted of an earth and stone wall constructed by the Romans, but now re-constructed by J.C.B.s!

Cross a stile and follow the top of the sea wall. Just below is a small sand and pebble beach which is exposed at low tide.

On reaching a brick building, turn right. Go through a metal gate and follow a gravel track, passing Outfall cottage. On your right is a green "mint sauce" filled reen. Directly ahead can be seen the summit of Twm Barlwm. When the track meets a road, turn right and follow it for about a mile and ponder on the extent of this area of land reclaimed from the sea by the Romans so long ago and the misery caused by the Great Flood of 1606 when their sea wall collapsed. (Also see Route 30).

The "mint sauce" on the right is known as Sealand Reen. To visit the leaning church of St Bride's, turn left past the Church House Inn.

This fine church with its tipsy tower is now unfortunately derelict. Some fascinating gargoyles and stone figures look down from the tower. A plaque in the porch commemorates the Great Flood of 1606.

Retrace your steps to the road junction and turn left along the road. Shortly, turn right by a F.P. sign (Foreshore 0.8 km) and over a footbridge spanning a reen to follow a hedge on the left. Two footbridges are crossed, then go left along a cart track and shortly go right over another footbridge and through the next field. Keep the hedge on your left as far as a stile. Turn right after the stile and follow the road back to the start.

ROUTE 32
THE BISHOPS' WALK (3 hours)

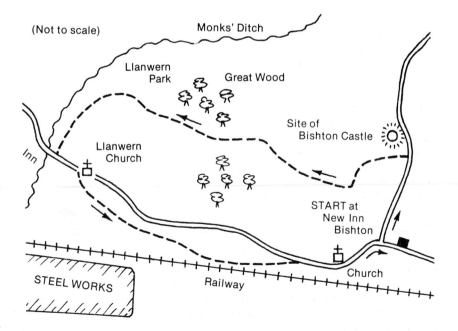

*"Bishton, as now written, would be more correctly
Bishopston, taking its name from the bishoprick of
Llandaff, to which See the parish has from time immemorial
been attached."*

Sir Joseph Bradney (1901)

Start from the New Inn near Bishton village (G.R. 392875). Walk north west to a road junction and turn right into Bishton village, to the post office. Turn left along a lane.

Across to the right, a low mound adjoining Castle Farm is all that remains of Bishton Castle. Originally known as Llangadwaladr's Castle, in due course the name was shortened to Lanke's Castle. It became a residence of the Bishops of Llandaff and the village subsequently became known as Bishops' town.

On reaching a bend in the road, go through the second of two adjoining metal gates and follow a hedge on the left to a stile. Ahead can be seen the giant Llanwern Steel Works, with its blast furnaces belching out smoke and steam to the sky. A stile can be seen at the end of the field. Do not go over it, but turn right and, keeping a hedge on your left, head for a stile at the top of the field.

To the right can be seen the twin hills of Wentwood and behind rises Wilcrick hill fort from which Cromwell's cannons bombarded Bishton Castle during the Civil War.

Go over the stile and keep the hedge on your left to the corner of the field. Follow the hedge to the right to a wooden hunting gate. Pass through it and descend into a valley, keeping a wood on your right, to a stile in the corner of the field.

Cross the stream (Llan Allen Winter Sewer — What a name for a babbling brook!) and head straight up to an oak tree framed in a hedge gap.

Now go left, following the edge of the wood to a metal gate and, shortly after, a wooden stile. Follow a fence to the right and go through a gap into the next field. Keep right, passing the edge of Great Wood, and descend into Llanwern Park where a large country house once stood. At one time it was owned by the Le Wallensis family who sold the property in the mid-17th century to Lewis Van of Coldra.

Directly ahead is a large barn. Head across the park for this building, following a path. Go over a stile in the right hand corner of the field and cross a small footbridge. Keep the hedge on your left as far as a metal gate. Pass through and go directly across a driveway and down a field.

Look up to the left to see the remains of a gateway to Llanwern House, which was a dignified Georgian house of three storeys owned by Lord Rhondda. A modern bungalow now stands on this site.

Llanwern House from an old painting

Soon you will reach a metal gate on the left. Go through and directly across the field, passing beneath some high voltage wires to a stile.

The reen below, to the right, is known as the Monk's Ditch, an incredible feat of engineering carried out by the monks from the long vanished Goldcliff Priory. For six centuries this watercourse has been in operation, helping to drain this area that was reclaimed from the sea by the Romans.

Cross the next field to a metal gate and over another field towards a metal gate and a road. Turn left and follow the road to Llanwern Church. The remains of an ancient stone cross can be seen in the churchyard, but the door to the church is generally kept locked.

Turn left down a lane beside the church and shortly turn left through a metal gate. Continue through some fields, keeping a hedge on your left and Llanwern Steel Works constantly on your right. Go through three metal gates down to the lower field. Cut down to the bottom corner of the field and cross a stream. Follow a fence on your right to a road through a metal gate just before Bishton Church.

This church is dedicated to St Cadwaladr (canonised in 688), who was the last of the ancient Welsh princes to rejoice in the title "King of Britain". The embattled 13th century tower is furnished with a small turret and strange gargoyles.

Turn right and follow the road back to the New Inn.

ROUTE 33
REDWICK ROUNDABOUT
(1½ hours)

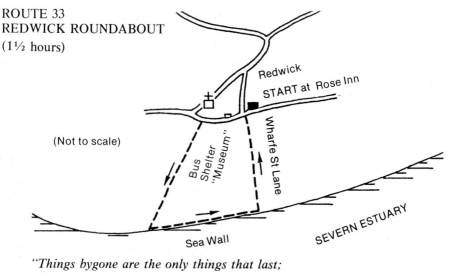

"Things bygone are the only things that last;
The present is mere grass quick mown away;
The past is stone and stands forever fast."

L. Hamilton

A short walk exploring the environs of Redwick village.

Start from the village hall car park which conveniently adjoins the Rose Inn (G.R. 413842).

First examine the unique bus shelter which was built by a local craftsman, using some fascinating pieces of stone that he has collected over the years. There are so many items of interest in the walls of this building that it is not possible to mention them all here. Inside, are two cider presses and a plaque on the wall informs the visitor that the building was designed and built by Mr Hubert Jones of "Jesmond", Redwick. In addition, the Prince of Wales Award 1979 plaque is also on display.

A glass fronted cavity in one wall contains a collection of interesting items found locally: Part of the skull of an ox "with tips of horns removed to be ground to powder for sale as an aphrodisiac — like the horns of the rhinocerous are today in Hong Kong and Singapore". There is also a wooden platter, tiles and other pot pieces found in the silt on the foreshore at Magor and Redwick Pill.

The cider presses came from Bryn Farm and, outside the shelter, can be seen boundary stones from the Duke of Beaufort's estate and a giant size stone "rolling pin" obtained from a blacksmith at Llanmartin.

Nearby is a stone stile with an inscription that has four spelling mistakes. Apparently the stone mason was working at the King's Head (a one-time Redwick pub) at the time and was rather drunk.

A set of stocks nearby look deceptively mediaeval, but they too were constructed a few years ago by the industrious Mr Hubert Jones.

The Stocks at Redwick and Hubert Jones who constructed them

Go through a gate into the churchyard. On the front of the porch of this fine old church is an inscription — "Great Flood of 1606" — and a strip of brass set into a plug of lead showing the level reached by the flood water.

Redwick Church over the years has changed its allegiance amongst several saints. In 1545 it was the church of St Michael the Archangel, in 1865 it was called St Mary's and in 1875 it was changed to St Thomas the Apostle.

The village of Redwick was developed by monks from Tintern Abbey in about 1100. They constructed the church utilising local labour. It is of interest that the stone was shipped over from Somerset. It suffered in 1402 at the hands of Owain Glyndwr's men and the fine stone altar and part of the rood loft was destroyed during the Civil War by Comwell's army.

In 1875 the church was considerably restored, but damaged once more in 1942 by German bombs and repaired three years later.

Leaving the church, go through a gate at the rear of the churchyard and turn left along the road to a footpath on the right (signposted Seawall 0.8 km). Pass through a metal gate and follow a vague path through the fields to a metal gate, over a stile and through a gap in a hedge. Go through a gate and cross a bridge over a wide reen to reach a metal gate. Then bear left to a wooden gate and up to the top of the sea wall and follow it to the left.

Ahead to the right can be seen Denny Island and to the left is Wentwood Forest and Gray Hill. Soon, below, may be seen a salmon fishery, utilising conical baskets supported on wooden trestles, similar to the one at Goldcliff. At this point (by a stile), go down to a metal gate and follow a gravel path, known as Wharfe Street Lane, back to Redwick.

Cobbler's Plain
and Trellech Ridge

*"The great ridge which stretches from Devauden to Trellech
and beyond forms the skyline. In the undulating country
between us and the ridge are hidden the little places we
know so well — Llangwm, Llansoy, the Star Pitch,
Cwmcarvan, and the rest — sleeping in the loveliest
maze of lanes and brooks and forming focal points in a
design of fields, hedges and copses as satisfying in form
as it is captivating in colour."*

Fred J. Hando
"Journeys in Gwent" (1951)

Trellech Churchyard, Preaching Cross and "Druid's Altar"

This is the area bounded by the A449 to the west, the B235 to the south and the
B4293 to the east. It contains the ridge of Cobbler's Plain and Trellech,
Chepstow Park Wood, Cwmcarvan Hill, Gaer Fawr, the sleepy villages of
Devauden, Llangwm and Mitchell Troy. It is a land of hill forts, curious
churches, quiet hamlets, meandering brooks and extensive views.

ROUTE 34
STAR HILL (2½ hours)

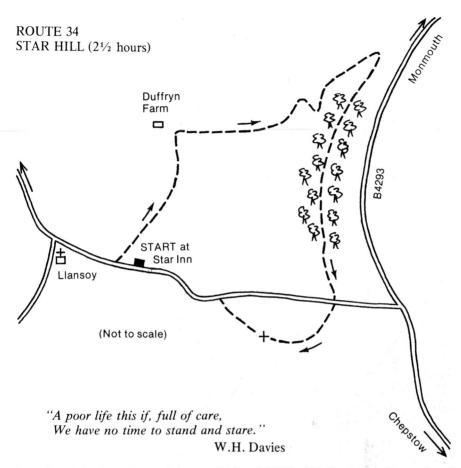

"A poor life this if, full of care,
We have no time to stand and stare."

W.H. Davies

Start from the Star Inn at Llansoy (G.R. 459023). Walk down the road and shortly turn right over a cattle grid and up Duffryn Farm drive. The lane soon descends into a valley.

Go through a metal gate and turn right to another metal gate and follow a cart track, keeping left of the barns and passing a solitary oak tree. On reaching another metal gate, go through and follow a hedge on the right to a metal gate at the top right hand corner of the field. Go through it and follow a hedge on the left and turn diagonally right up to a ruined cottage. On its left side, turn left and go through a gap in a hedge. Keep straight on to a fence on the left. Follow this fence along a well worn path. Directly ahead on the ridge can be seen St Dennis' Church at Llanishen.

Join a cart track and go through a metal gate on to a gravel track. On meeting a road, turn immediately right along a cart track leading through the trees. Keep right of a square stone construction and follow a path between hedges to soon descend through a wood. Follow the edge of the wood with views of north Gwent on the right.

On joining a road, go downhill past Tor-y-Mynydd and follow a green lane between high hedges to join the road by a farm. Turn right and after a few hundred yards take the road on the left. Follow this to Church Farm. (Or, if you have had enough, go straight down the road to the Star Inn).

Go through a metal gate on the right and down to the church. The main feature of interest in this little church is the rather fine "barrel" ceiling.

Behind the church, go over a stile and follow a hedge on the right to a wooden gate. Turn left and follow the road back to the start.

ROUTE 35
TOUR OF TRELLECH
(1 hour)

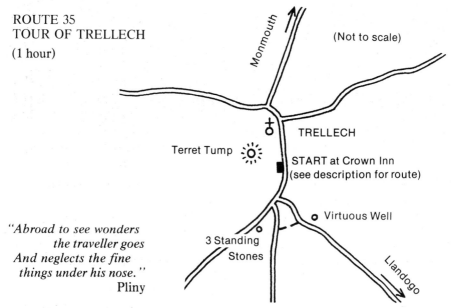

"Abroad to see wonders
the traveller goes
And neglects the fine
things under his nose."
Pliny

Start at the Crown Inn (G.R. 501054). Go into the yard behind the inn and look left over a gate to see a high mound some 50 yards away. This mound is called the Terret Tump, believed to be the earthworks of an early Norman motte and bailey castle. It has also been suggested that this site is the burial place of a large number of King Harold's men who were killed in a local battle.

Walk into the churchyard where you will see an ancient preaching cross and the so-called Druid's Altar, a huge slab of stone.

The church is very large for such a small village, perhaps indicating that Trellech was once a place of greater importance. It has a fine Early English Nave and the tower at the west end is crowned by a lofty stone spire.

Inside the church is a very interesting sundial. It was previously kept in the village and was presented by Lady Magdalen Probert in 1689 to record some of the outstanding features of the village. The base is a sort of stone guide book. One side shows a carving of Trellech's three standing stones with their height measurements shown on each stone: 8 ft, 10 ft and 14 ft.

Sundial at Trellech Church   *Harold's Stones, Trellech*

Latin inscriptions give the following information (with literal translation):

> *MAIOR SAXIS* (Greater in regard to the stones)
> *HIC FUIT VICTOR HARALDUS* (Harold the Conqueror was here)

This possibly refers to Harold's supposed victory and the belief that the three stones were erected as his memorial.

Another side shows the Trellech Tump which is given the inscription:

> *MAGNA MOLE* (Great in regard to the mound)
> *O QUOT HIC SEPULTI* (Oh how many are buried here).

This seems to support the one time belief that the mound was constructed as a burial tomb. According to local legend a great calamity will befall anyone who attempts to excavate the mound.

A third side of the sundial base shows the Virtuous Well, which is situated just outside Trellech and was once famous for its healing powers.

> *MAXIMA FONTE* (Greatest regard to the well)
> *DOM MAGD. PROBERT OSTENDIT* (Lady Magdalen Probert gives proof of it)

The fourth side is blank.   When the pedestal was removed from the school garden, where it was originally sited, it was found that the base was the ancient church font, inverted.

Leave the churchyard by the main gate and pass the Crown Inn to follow the B4293 (right) towards Llanishen. About 200 yards from the road junction, a kissing gate on the left gives access to a field where the three standing stones can be seen.

They point to the sky at a crazy angle and are sometimes referred to as "Harold's Stones". It is claimed that they were erected to glorify his victory over the Britons. However, it is more likely that they were standing here centuries before he came to Gwent. They are composed of "pudding stone", a kind of stone made up of hard pebbles enclosed in a cement-like rock. It has been suggested that they were once part of a Druidical Circle, but as they are in a straight line it does not seem very likely. They are also supposed to have been thrown here by Jack of Kent, in a fit of temper, from the summit of Skirrid Fawr which, as the stone flies, is about twelve miles away.

Return to the road junction. Turn right and immediately left to follow the Llandogo road for about 250 yards until you reach a metal gate on the left giving access to the "Virtuous Well".

This was originally called St Anne's Well, but later became known as the "Virtuous Well" because of its "medicinal virtues".

"A chalybeat spring issuing beneath an antiquated arch.
The spring is strongly impregnated with carbonate of iron,
and is considered efficacious in cases of debility, dyspepsia
and hypochondriasis."

It was also used as a Wishing Well — a visitor would take a pebble and, dropping it quietly into the water, would at the same time make a wish. If plenty of bubbles appeared, the wish would be granted, if moderately few there would be a delay in obtaining the wish, and if there were no bubbles at all the wish would not be realised.

Return to the road and turn left, then immediately right to follow a bridleway (signposted Catbrook Road 0.2 km). On reaching the road, turn right and head back to the start.

The Virtuous Well, Trellech

ROUTE 36
KILGWRRG AND WOLVESNEWTON
(3 hours)

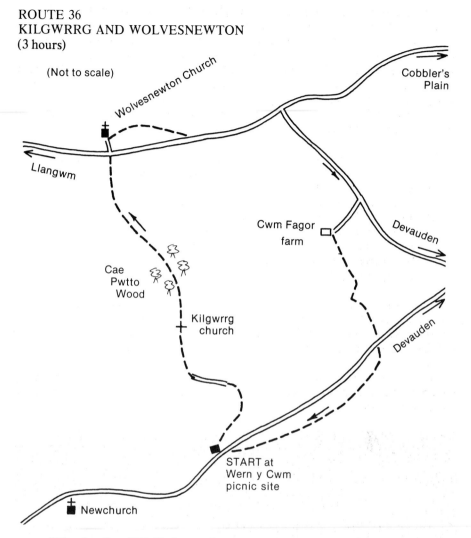

(Not to scale)

Wolvesnewton Church

Cobbler's Plain

Llangwm

Cwm Fagor farm

Devauden

Cae Pwtto Wood

Kilgwrrg church

Devauden

START at Wern y Cwm picnic site

Newchurch

"The family of Wolf, from whom the parish takes its name, were said to have been resident here from the first to the sixteenth century."

Sir Joseph Bradney

Start from Wern-y-cwm Picnic Site which is situated on the Devauden to Newchurch road (G.R. 468977).

Follow a gravel track from near the entrance to the picnic site to reach a bend. Then keep straight on to follow a path down through the trees.

On reaching a clearing, you will obtain a pleasant view down into a valley of green fields with Kilgwrrwg Church directly below. Continue along the track to shortly pass through a field and then ascend slightly to join a tarmac lane. Turn left and go down hill to pass Kilgwrrwg Farm (a listed building, but unfortunately modernised with cement rendering etc.).

Go through a gate and past the rear of the house to cross a field and reach a wooden footbridge. Ascend a field to reach the church.

This is one of the smallest and remotest churches in Gwent, but it is still regularly used for worship. It is situated in a small circular churchyard in the middle of a field.

An interesting feature is the slim Celtic Cross. Also of interest, in the chuchyard, is a war grave which records the death of a soldier on the last day of World War I. He is said to have been the last soldier to be killed in that war.

R. Morgan
Able Seaman R.N.
H.M.S. Garland
11th Nov 1918 age 26.

The double bell turret on the west gable of the church retains its original bell dated 1698 and it was made in Chepstow by Evan Evans who was a well known Bell Founder at that time.

Behind the church descend the field, bearing slightly left to cross a stream and go through a little wooden gate. Follow the hedge on the left to reach a large open area. Directly ahead you will see a stile giving access into a wood. Follow a path winding pleasantly through the trees to reach a metal gate. From here follow a hedge on the left down to a gate. Then on to another gate, across a stream, past a barn, to a gate. Now, following a cart track, cross another stream and up to a road junction. Go straight across and follow a road leading to Wolvesnewton Church.

This attractive church is dedicated to St Thomas a Becket who was murdered in Canterbury Cathedral in 1170. It was founded in the 12th century, but probably only the font dates back to that time.

During the 15th century, the church was enlarged and given a new chancel and a belfry stage with a saddleback roof to its tower. Unfortunately, the extra weight has caused the tower to lean, making the belfry now rather crooked on its top.

The stained glass windows are of special interest. One of them depicts the Arthurian legend of Sir Galahad and the Holy Grail. But perhaps the greatest treasure held by this church is the Elizabethan Chalice and cover dating from 1586. It is still used at the celebration of the Holy Communion and it is claimed to be the largest Elizabethan Communion Cup in Wales.

After examining the church, turn left outside the entrance gates and follow a grass lane past a ruined building on the left (once an inn called The Fox and Hounds). Shortly, go right through a gate and follow a hedge on the right to reach a gate in the corner of the field. Head straight on to find a gate in the bottom left hand corner of the field, near a stream and giving access to a road. Turn left and follow this road through the peaceful valley of Wolvesnewton. This name suggests that there was once an abundance of savage wolves troubling this locality, but the name in fact comes from the family Wolf who for centuries were Lords of this vicinity. Their residence was on the earthworks to the north west of the church where a farmhouse called Cwrt-y-gaer now stands. The mound occupies approximately one and a half acres and is circular with a moat on the south and west sides.

Turn up a lane to the right, just before reaching Great House Farm. This traffic free (usually!) lane ascends the side of the valley with very fine views towards northern Gwent. After about a mile, turn right towards Cwm Vagor Farm and go through a gate on the left (just before a barn) and then go up to another gate. Then head straight up across a field to reach a stile and then up to a path which climbs through the woods to pass a riding stables. On reaching a gravel track, turn left and then straight on to a road and over a cross roads to follow a lane leading back to the starting point.

ROUTE 37
LLANGWM ISAF AND LLANGWM UCHAF (1½ hours)

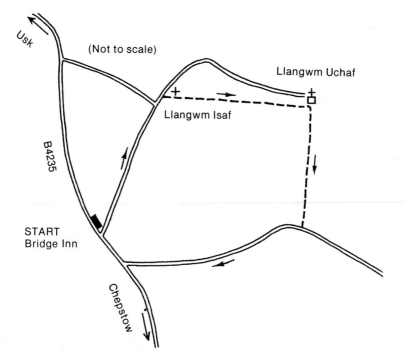

"How many, I wonder, have seen the two churches, the valley itself, the Pentre, the Court farm, the mill, the camps, the Pwll or any of the other joys which render Llangwm one of our most fascinating hamlets?"

Fred J. Hando

A short circular walk visiting the two churches of Llangwm Isaf and Llangwm Uchaf. Start from the Bridge Inn at Llangwm on the B4235 (G.R. 427002).

Walk down the road past the side of the inn to pass a farm and then go through a kissing gate giving access to the church of Llangwm Isaf (Lower church in the dingle) which is dedicated to St John.

This is the sister church to Llangwm Uchaf and is a 19th century building, known locally as the Little Church. The two churches are both in one parish and these days they generally have the same congregation.

At the rear of the church is a stile. Cross it and continue to another stile, then across the next field and through a gate. The path then crosses a brook and enters Llangwm Uchaf (higher church in the dingle) churchyard through a metal kissing gate.

This very fine church, hidden in a secluded valley, contains a remarkable mediaeval screen complete with its original rood loft. Dedicated to St Jerome, the church is mainly 13th century with an embattled tower on the north side of the chancel. The nave is relatively modern and has an attractive barrel roof.

On the chancel arch can be seen a carving depicting a man's head with foliage down both sides. It is known as the Green Man.

In front of the chancel arch and across the entire width of the church is the mediaeval screen with its roof loft, all richly and delicately carved with patterns of foliage and flowing shapes. It is a very fine example of 15th century craftsmanship and is believed to be the work of local men. The only screen in Wales comparable with this one is at Llananno in Powys.

The screen at Llangwm was restored in 1970 by J.P. Seddon, who renewed the red, blue and green colouring and also designed the wooden lectern and the stained glass east window.

The tall tower houses three bells which were cast by John Palmer of Gloucester in the 17th century.

From the church porch, go through a metal gate directly opposite to cross a stream and head straight up a field, past a lone tree to reach a wooden gate in the hedge. Then cross the next field to another gate and turn left along a farm drive. Now turn right on a tarmac road which is followed back to the starting point.

Wye Valley

*"O Sylvan Wye! thou wanderer through the woods
How often has my spirit turned to thee!"*

William Wordsworth

Tintern Abbey   *19th century engraving*

This final section of Gwent to be explored is probably the most famous part of the county. It contains the winding river Wye between Chepstow and Monmouth and the narrow secluded valleys on its west flank. Across the water is England which was once regarded as "no-man's land". Anyone entering from Gwent was liable to lose an arm and be cast into the Wye.

In this area you may explore the ruins of Chepstow Castle and Tintern Abbey, or visit the Piercefield Walks, the 365 Steps, the Kymin Naval Temple, the Suck Stone and the Buckstone and the sites of early industries.

ROUTE 38
KYMIN HILL AND BUNJUPS WOOD (3½ hours)

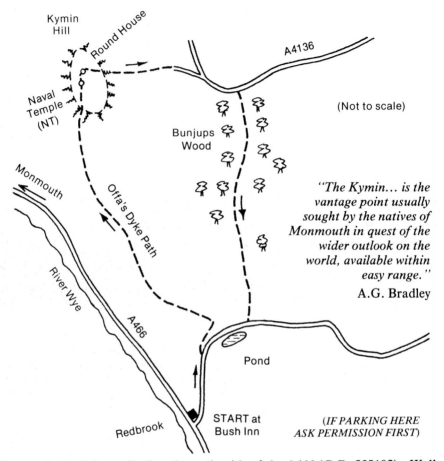

"The Kymin... is the vantage point usually sought by the natives of Monmouth in quest of the wider outlook on the world, available within easy range."

A.G. Bradley

Start at the Bush Inn at Redbrook, on the side of the A466 (G.R. 535102). Walk past the inn up the Newland Road (B4231) to pass under a very unusual incline bridge (scheduled as an Ancient Monument).

Further on you may notice on the right a derelict inn (bearing the faded lettering — IND COOPE BURTON ALES). This inn is still shown on the 2½-inch map and must have caught out many thirsty walkers.

Take a turning on the left, past the rear of a cottage. Keep straight on at the junction. The metalled track climbs the hillside and shortly Offa's Dyke Path links in from the right. Past a farmhouse, the track becomes a leafy lane overhung by holly. Go through a metal gate and straight on, following Offa's Dyke Path waymarks. The views are now more open, looking out across to

Penallt in the Wye Valley and Bunjups Wood. Traverse a stile, a metal gate, a stile, and turn left, crossing the next two stiles.

Notice heaps of Conglomerate rocks in the woods on the left. Conglomerate is a particular feature of this area, which is sometimes referred to as "Pudding Stone Country". On to a stile and through two kissing gates to a National Trust car park (one can of course drive to this point from the A4136). Now head up to the Naval Temple.

The Naval Temple, Kymin Hill

This was constructed in 1800 following the second anniversary of the Battle of the Nile in appreciation of the sixteen admirals who had won important victories during the late 18th century. Medallions can be seen commemorating the following admirals and the dates of the victories with which they were associated: Thompson, Duncan, Boscowen, Hood, Howe, Warren, Gell, Nelson, St Vincent, Rodney, Hawke, Bridport, Cornwallis, Parker, Keith and Mitchell.

Nelson, accompanied by Sir William and Lady Hamilton, visited Monmouth in 1802. They travelled by boat from Ross-on-Wye. When the boat came in sight, a cannon was fired from the Kymin Hill and Nelson's party was welcomed at the quayside by the Mayor and the town band.

A few days later, Nelson visited the Round House, also on Kymin Hill, where he had breakfast and admired the view which he declared to be one of the finest he had ever seen. He also admired the Naval Temple and said that it was *"the only monument of its kind erected to the English Navy in the Kingdom"*.

The Round House is a white tower further up from the Naval Temple. From here is a very fine view to the north of Gwent, as mentioned by Nelson; it used to be claimed that nine counties could be seen from here. The Round House was erected in 1793 by a group of Monmouth gentlemen as a venue for holding weekly meetings and also as a summer house. Inside, they constructed a kitchen and a banqueting room. On the roof a powerful telescope was installed and a bowling green was later added nearby.

The Round House, Kymin Hill

From the Round House head down in a north easterly direction (leaving the Offa's Dyke Path) to corner of a field and go over a stile. Keep the fence on your right and descend to a stile and through the next field to a gate and the drive to Beaulieu Farm. Turn left and follow the lane down to the A4136.

Turn right and follow the main road for approximately 400 yards. Just inside the edge of the wood on the right and by a Forestry Commission sign is a footpath leading into the wood. After a stiff climb, a wide track is reached. Turn right and follow it down through Bunjups Wood, ignoring all side turnings. Bear left at the junction of tracks, keeping on the main path. Turn right at the next junction.

Shortly, where the track bears left, take a narrow path on the right (waymarked on a tree, but easily missed!). Descend through a dark wood along a well used path, occasionally waymarked with yellow arrows (Ramblers' Association trail).

The author met a young badger on this track one afternoon, who stared fascinated for about thirty seconds before scuttling away.

Keep going downwards over two junctions to a stile where the track crosses the route of an old railway line. Down to another stile, on to a metal gate and down to a road. Turn right and head back to Redbrook.

> *"About two miles from Monmouth is a small stream called*
> *Redbrook — where some iron and tinplate works give*
> *animation of the local scenery."*

Archdeacon William Coxe (1801)

ROUTE 39
THE BUCKSTONE AND SUCK STONE (3 hours)

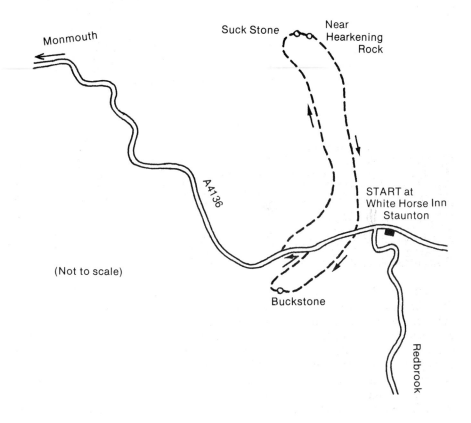

"Which the gentlest touch at once set moving,
But all earth's power couldn't cast it from its base."

Anon

Start from the White Horse Inn at Staunton on the A4136 (G.R. 548126). Follow the pavement along the Monmouth road and take a lane on the left to a waymarked path by a wooden gate. Turn right up a slope and follow the path beside a stone wall.

Soon you are looking down on Staunton village and across to the Forest of Dean. Below to the left can be seen the tower of Newland Church.

Go through a gap in the stone wall to the Buckstone. This hunk of rock is a mass of Conglomerate, or "Pudding Stone". As a geological feature it is older than the grey cliffs of carboniferous limestone which are such impressive features in the Lower Wye Valley.

At one time the Buckstone did indeed live up to its name and move. The Rev D Booker in the 18th century wrote:

> *"So exactly does this gigantic insulated rock seem to equilibrate that a spectator would almost suppose he could dislodge it from its narrow base with the force of his single arm, and send it headlong down the steep declivity on which it stands. Such attempts have often been made by the united efforts of a number of stout young rustics and I have perceived it to gently move in a kind of rocking motion but invariably settling on its ancient pivot."*

The Buckstone   *19th century engraving*

However, on Wednesday 10th June 1885, the stone was completely overturned by a party of five strolling players (actors) who, in company with the landlord of the Agincourt Inn, went from Monmouth to visit this ancient rock. Two of the company climbed to the top and, while in this position, the other members commenced to push the boulder, then suddenly they were surprised to see the large mass turn half round and the next moment it toppled and descended a distance of about ten yards down the hill. The two men on top saved themselves from being crushed to death by jumping clear.

Throughout the neighbourhood this incident caused great indignation and the matter was brought to the attention of the government, with the result that in a short time steps were taken to collect the fragments and the stone was successfully re-erected in its former position. But unfortunately it no longer rocks.

A certain Dr Dyke in the 19th century claimed that the Buckstone was the remains of a Druidical altar. Before battle the Britons would gather round the rock and the priest foretold their fate by the sound obtained when the Chiefs struck their shields against the rock. He whose blow was the loudest was declared the leader of the adventure.

There is an interesting hunk of rock on the east side of the Buckstone. Its centre has been scooped out to form a basin with a channel, seemingly to let out liquid contents which have variously supposed to have been water, wine or the blood of Druidical sacrifices!

The view from here is perhaps even finer than that from Kymin Hill, as it takes in the Malvern Hills, Forest of Dean and, in clear weather, the Clee Hills of Shropshire.

Follow the path to the west (past "Take your Litter Home" sign) and after a few yards turn sharp right by a dead tree. Go down a track through rock strewn woods to a broad track. Turn right and go gently downhill to the main road. Cross the road and turn left following the grass verge for about a quarter of a mile to a layby. Here, turn sharp right along a forest track to pass through High Meadow Woods. At a junction, turn right.

After about a mile you will see a very large flat faced boulder directly ahead. This is known as the Suck Stone. Directly below it, a well worn path leads up to the rock. It is reputed to be the largest piece of detached Conglomerate rock in England and Wales and must weigh about 14,000 tons.

The Suck Stone

The Near Hearkening Rock

A Scrambler's Challenge

Climb on to the Suck Stone at the bottom right hand corner without any assistance from your companion. This is a feat of climbing skill and arm strength. Many try and fail. The angle of the slab above is quite shallow and you can gain the "summit" easily, but take care on the descent.

Follow a waymarked path to the right of the Suck Stone and climb steeply through the trees to the Near Hearkening Rock. Turn left below the enormous overhang (good place to shelter in the rain and have lunch).

It is said that at one time the local gamekeepers used to use this rock as an observation platform and listening post (hence the name) when they were trying to locate poachers moving around in the woods below.

The path leads around a corner and up to the top of the rock for superb views towards Monmouth, the Black Mountains and the surrounding woodland.

Follow a waymarked path. Turn right at the next junction and follow a gravel track past Reddings Lodge. Extensive views on the right to the Black Mountains, Sugar Loaf and Skirrid. Carry on past a housing estate to the main road and White Horse Inn.

ROUTE 40
PENALLT CHURCH (3½ hours)

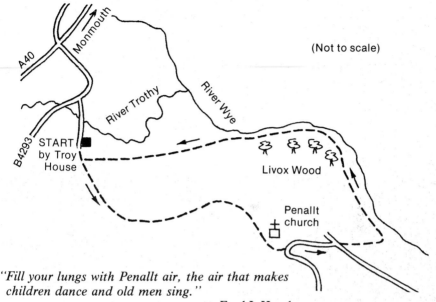

"Fill your lungs with Penallt air, the air that makes children dance and old men sing."

Fred J. Hando

Park in the lane near the entrance to Troy House (G.R. 508114). This lane is reached by turning off the B4293 just south of Monmouth.

Follow the lane past a farm and through a covered area. Go straight on past a silo tower, through a metal gate and on for a few hundred yards to a metal gate on the right. Go through and follow the left hand side of the field. At the top left corner of the field, by an oak tree, enter the next field and head diagonally across it to the top left corner. Looking back, you will see good views of Monmouth town.

Cross two stiles in quick succession and then turn left along a broad track. After approximately 50 yards turn right and follow a path leading up through the woods. Where the track bends sharply right, go straight on and shortly turn right. After about 100 yards you will reach a gate at the end of the wood.

Go through the gate and follow the left side of the next two fields. From here, there are fine views down into the Wye Valley and across to Kymin Hill. Pass through a wooden gate and below a small barn. Keep right of the next gate, then uphill slightly and bear left by a telegraph pole (track easily missed), following a narrow track past a white cottage. Turn left and make for the church.

To the left of a footpath sign is an old stone mounting block, once used by the gentry to help them climb onto their horses' backs.

Penallt Church

Penallt Church dates back to the 12th century, but it was drastically restored in 1887. In the churchyard is the base and part of the shaft of a 15th century preaching cross.

Inside the chuch are a variety of interesting items. The heavy oak door is carved with the date 1532 and on the west wall can be seen the Royal Arms of Queen Anne dated 1709.

A Belgian refugee, during the First World War, was responsible for carving the High Altar as a copy of one at Ravenna. Of particular antiquity is a very old oak chest, carved out of a solid tree, known as St Beuno's chest.

After visiting the church, go back to the F.P. sign and descend the road past a telephone box for about a quarter of a mile. Just past a drive to a cottage on the left (opposite a metal gate and a small barn), turn left and go down a track between ivy and moss covered stone walls.

Where the path emerges from the trees to join a broad track, turn *immediately* left (easily missed) and down through Lower Wood to the river. Turn left over a stile and follow the bank. This is millstone country and at low water round stones may be seen lying on the river bed. Penallt, with its outcrops of Quartz Conglomerate, was renowned in the 19th century for the production of high quality millstones and grindstones. They were transported by river to Chepstow and then exported to North Devon and Ireland.

An elderly couple in a little cottage at Penallt told me of their grandfather, the last millstone maker of Penallt, who used to take his stones by barge down the Wye and across to Bristol, and then walk home to Penallt from Chepstow — a distance of some 12 miles.

Continue along the river bank, crossing three stiles at well spaced intervals, then follow the edge of Livox Wood to a stile as you come out of the trees. Keep straight across a field and ascend sloping ground on the left, following a narrow track which becomes broader and leads back to Troy House and your starting point.

The original part of Troy House dates back to the 14th century and there may well have been an earlier building on this site. According to Adam of Usk, there was a Phillip Scudamore of Troy who was hanged at Shrewsbury in 1411 for being in league with Owain Glyndwr.

In the reign of Henry VII, Troy was the seat of Sir William Herbert. However, in about 1600 the Earl of Worcester purchased the estate and brought it into the Somerset family. They became dissatisfied with the front of the building and commissioned Inigo Jones, the most famous architect in the land, to redesign the north side. The magnificence of his work may be appreciated today.

It is said that at one time the house contained the cradle of Henry V (he was born in Monmouth Castle) and the sword that he used at the Battle of Agincourt. Troy House has been used as a Convent and last served as a special school for girls. It is now private property.

ROUTE 41
CLEDDON SHOOTS
(2 hours)

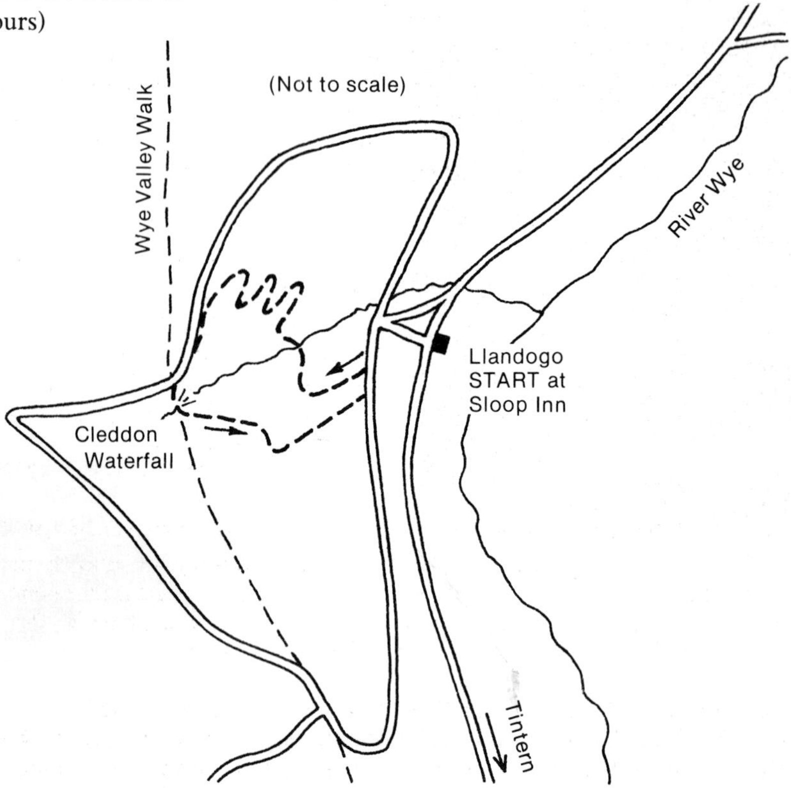

(Not to scale)

Wye Valley Walk

River Wye

Llandogo
START at
Sloop Inn

Cleddon
Waterfall

Tintern

> *"Delightful village! One by one*
> *Its climbing dwellings caught the sun*
> *So bright the scene, the air so clear*
> *Young love and joy seem'd stationed here."*
>
> Robert Bloomfield

Start from the Sloop Inn at Llandogo (G.R. 526042). If using the car park, ask permission at the inn to leave your car.

Go up the road opposite the inn. Turn left at a road junction and follow road to pass a stream on the right tumbling down from the Cleddon Gorge. Just around the corner is a F.P. sign (Cleddon Falls and Shoots). Turn right to follow a leafy lane leading up beside a stone wall, passing old stone cottages. The view of the river and valley improves as more height is gained. In due course the track becomes a surfaced path, but after about ten yards turn right to enter the picturesque Cleddon Gorge along a broad shelf, traversing the sides of a deep valley.

Cross the stream by moss covered boulders and then walk along the other side of the gorge and through the woods above Llandogo, to shortly find a path on the left. This climbs the wooded slopes above in a series of long zig zags which are particularly beautiful when carpeted with autumn leaves.

This long series of zig zags provide a very easy ascent to the top and is in fact part of a now forgotten 19th century Tourist Path.

"A circuitous path has been lately made from the village up to this waterfall, and a guide is appointed to show it after the manner of the Wyndcliff walks."

19th century Guide Book

Cleddon Shoots after heavy rain (note the icicles)

A stile is reached and then the falls are within earshot and shortly in sight. Make for the small clearing by the road, where it is easy to scramble down (with care on the loose leaves) to see the falls. The best time to come here is after heavy rain, as normally the falls are not particularly impressive.

Turn left past a Bridleway sign (Tintern 1.6 km) to follow a brief section of the Wye Valley Walk. Shortly, turn left at junction, following a wide track down, passing a pink cottage with minute windows, and on down a leafy path. This descends pleasantly through the woods with the Wye glinting below. Ignore a steep track on the right and continue beside a rambling stone wall to reach a flight of stone steps, descending steeply to a surfaced track. Turn left and shortly rejoin the original route leading back to the Sloop Inn.

The name of this inn gives a reminder of the old shipping days when Llandogo was once a busy river port. It is believed that the name, Llandogo, is derived from Odoceus — a Bishop of Llandaff in the 6th century who owned a house on the hillside near the Cleddon stream.

ROUTE 42
THE LOWER WYE VALLEY WALK (Allow 2—3 days to reach Hereford)
(For Map see page 138)

This 40 mile route starts from the car park at Chepstow Leisure Centre and is waymarked throughout its length to Ross-on-Wye. It passes through Piercefield Park (see Route 44), Wynd Cliff, Tintern, Llandogo, Redbrook, past Monmouth, Dixton Church, across the Biblins suspension bridge, Symonds Yat East, Kerne Bridge and over Chase Wood to Ross-on-Wye.

The route then continues to Hereford. It is hoped that one day a route will be established all the way to the source of the Wye on Plynlimon Mountain.

Strip maps and a detailed description of the route may be obtained from the Public Relations Officer, Gwent County Council, County Hall, Cwmbrân, Gwent.

ROUTE 43
THE PIERCEFIELD WALKS (2½ hours)

> *"Winding Walks through wood and glade lead from point*
> *to point, and at every one some further gem of river-*
> *scenery is disclosed..."*
>
> A.G. Bradley

This is a linear walk which can either be undertaken as an "out and back" route or you can arrange with a friend to have a car at each end of the journey.

Start at the Chepstow Leisure Centre car park near St Kingsmark school (G.R. 528943). The route in fact follows the initial section of the Wye Valley Walk and is waymarked with yellow dotted arrows.

In the middle of the 18th century, the first tourists during this new age of "Romantic Wandering" came to the Wye Valley to visit the Piercefield estate which at that time was the home of Valentine Morris. He was probably the first person to attempt to commercialise the area. To tempt the visitor, he set out the grounds of his estate with ten named views — The Pleasant View, The Alcove, The Grotto, The Double View, The Great Beech Tree, The Giant's Cave, The Top of the Hill, Lover's Leap, The Temple and the Wyndcliff. He opened the grounds to the public two days a week and visitors were escorted for a small charge by a resident guide around the viewpoints.

Valentine Morris left Piercefield in 1772 and returned to Antigua, where he had spent his early childhood. He later became Lieutenant Governor of the Island of St Vincent, but he was to suffer various misfortunes including a term of imprisonment. Piercefield was sold in 1784 for £26,000 to pay off debts and Valentine Morris went to live with friends in Jersey. In 1789 he died in London while staying with his sister in Bloomsbury Square.

He will always be remembered for his once famous Piercefield Walks, although certain sections of the Walks have now virtually disappeared and the viewpoints are of little consequence due to trees obscuring the views. However the main path connecting the old viewpoints has been cleared (by the efforts of the Wye Valley Warden Service and Forestry Commission) and now forms part of the popular Wye Valley Walk.

Originally the walks began at "The Alcove" which was at the Chepstow end of the estate. This was a lookout point where the visitors could sit on the edge of the cliff and gaze at the Wye and Chepstow Castle. From there the walk led past "The Platform" and other viewpoints to "The Grotto". This was a small cave decorated with stones and metals of various colours.

ROUTE 43

(Not to scale)

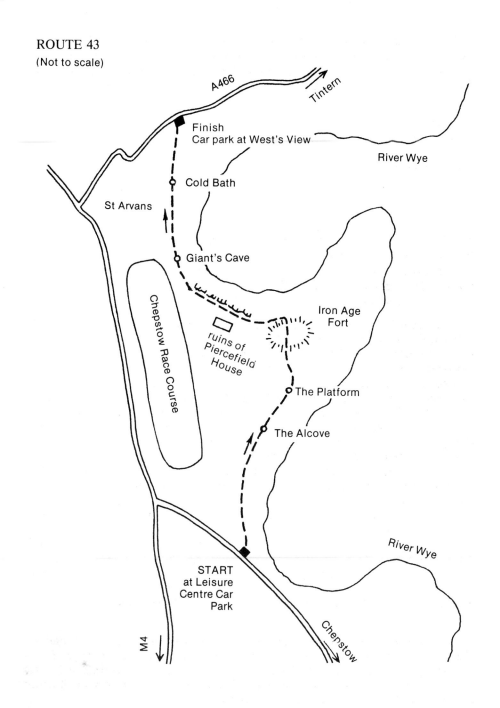

A466

Tintern

Finish
Car park at West's View

River Wye

Cold Bath

St Arvans

Giant's Cave

Chepstow Race Course

ruins of
Piercefield
House

Iron Age
Fort

The Platform

The Alcove

START
at Leisure
Centre Car
Park

M4

Chepstow

River Wye

After this came "The Double View" which was once furnished with a "Chinese seat". At "The Halfway Seat", a "Great Beech Tree" provided a shady spot and a view of the Lancaut peninsula. This was follows by a visit to "The Druid's Temple", "The Pleasant View" and "The Giant's Cave". The path leading into the cave was guarded by a stone giant who appeared to crouch above the entrance holding a large rock which he threatened to drop on the visitor. However, through the course of time, frost damaged the giant's arms until he dropped the rock and later followed it down a steep bank to the river below.

The Giant's Cave, Piercefield Walks

From the Giant's Cave the Wye Valley Walk descends to a spot in the woods below known as "The Cold Bath" and then climbs by many steps to reach the Lower Wynd Cliff car park. Thus to visit Lover's Leap and The Temple site required a short detour from the present route.

After "The Giant's Cave" the walk then led to the "Top of the Hill" and the "Paradise Seat" which were two viewpoints on the edge of the cliff. Then on to "Lover's Leap" where the 150 ft drop is still guarded by iron railings.

John Byng visited this viewpoint in 1781 and wrote *"I have never heard that it was attempted: the first leap would cure the most heart felt pangs!"*

Near this point was a small building called "The Temple", which was said to be one of the finest viewpoints. It was demolished in about 1800 when the present road (A466) was constructed from St Arvans to Tintern, but the point is still known as Temple Doors.

The viewpoint on the Wynd Cliff was made the climax of the Piercefield Walks and in 1825, when the new road was built, the 365 Steps were also made. They are described in Route 45.

In 1926 the Piercefield estate took on a new identity when the Chepstow Race Course came into being. The grand old house was left empty for many years and during the Second World War it suffered at the hands of American troops who were stationed there and apparently used it for target practice. At the end of the war, racing recommenced and the mansion was left to decay, the Walks being used only by people who were fortunate to know of their existence.

ROUTE 44
THE 365 STEPS (1½ hours)

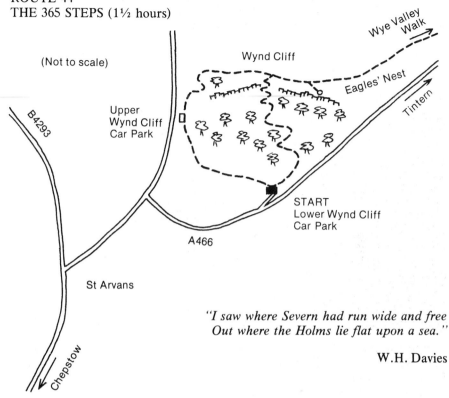

(Not to scale)

Wynd Cliff

Wye Valley Walk

Eagles' Nest

Tintern

B4293

Upper
Wynd Cliff
Car Park

START
Lower Wynd Cliff
Car Park

A466

St Arvans

Chepstow

"I saw where Severn had run wide and free
Out where the Holms lie flat upon a sea."

W.H. Davies

Start from the Lower Wynd Cliff car park (.G.R. 526973). This is located on the north side of the A466 (Chepstow to Monmouth road) below the Wynd Cliff and approximately one mile from St Arvans.

A map in the car park provides information on the location and route of the 365 Steps Walk.

From the car park walk past the information board and around a rocky corner to shortly go through the trees to reach the start of the steps.

Originally these steps started from the rear of Moss Cottage where tourists used to buy refreshments and then pay 6d. to walk up the steps to the top of the Wyndcliff. Inside the cottage was a large round table that was cut from a walnut tree taken from the grounds of Chepstow Castle. Unfortunately Moss Cottage fell into disuse and it was sadly demolished in about 1962. A bungalow near the site of this thatched cottage retains the old name.

The steps were constructed by the Duke of Beaufort's Steward, Osmond Wyatt, in 1828 and he probably built Moss Cottage as well. Before the Wye Valley road was constructed, the Wynd Cliff and its unique walk was part of the Piercefield estate.

Restoration of the Steps was carried out in 1972 by army apprentices from Beachley under a scheme initiated by the Lower Wye Valley Preservation Society. Further work has subsequently been carried out by the Wye Valley Warden Service and Gwent County Council footpath maintenance teams.

The Walk suffers occasionally from problems of windblown trees after gales which may obstruct the path, so go carefully.

Ahead, through the trees the Steps lead upwards, twisting around boulders of moss covered limestone. One passes through a split rock and then, with the cliffs looming steeply above, the Steps wind through a chaos of fallen boulders and ivy festooned trees. Huge chunks of limestone, pattered with ornate designs fashioned by water over thousands of years, serve as a reminder that the Wye was responsible for cutting this deep gorge through the hills as it pursued its course southwards to join the Severn.

As the path steepens, one is able to appreciate the height already attained and the fine view of the Wye through the trees. Above are some green iron railings and an old ship's ladder which bridges a gully and leads to a small platform where a good view is obtained and one can regain any lost breath. Then on up a short, but steep flight of very irregular concrete steps (laid down by the Army) and along a path to join with the route of the Wye Valley Walk.

Turn right along a wide track for a few hundred yards and then turn sharp right and descend to "The Eagle's Nest". This in itself is a fine piece of stonework, taking the form of a semi-circular box with a lower deck reached by stone steps. Perched on the very brink of the cliff, this look out point is more than 700 ft above the river.

Miss Gagg of Livox Farm arranged for this stone platform and grotto to be constructed in the 19th century and later there was even talk of building an observatory there as well. A drawing was published which showed the proposed tower, but due to a lack of financial support it was never built.

*View from the
Eagle's Nest
on the
Wynd Cliff*

136

The view from here is magnificent and before Local Government reorganisation, it was claimed that nine counties could be seen from here. The number is now probably reduced to five!

Fosbroke once wrote:

> *"What a cathedral is among churches, the Wyndcliff is among prospects. Like Snowdon, it ought to be visited at sunrise...*
> *It is not only magnificent, but so novel that it excites an involuntary start of astonishment; and so sublime that it elevates the mind into instantaneous rapture... The spectator stands upon the edge of a precipice, the depth of which is awful to contemplate, with the river winding at his feet."*

Go back up to the Wye Valley Walk and retrace your route past the path leading down to the 365 Steps and continue through the woods to reach the Upper Wynd Cliff car park (G.R. 524973). Turn left here and follow the yellow waymarks down some rustic steps and back to the starting point.

This route can of course be walked from the Upper Wynd Cliff car park to subsequently descend the 365 Steps, but this takes away much of the atmosphere and challenge of the route.

ROUTE 45
OFFA'S DYKE PATH — Sedbury to Monmouth (One strenuous day)

> *"There is a famous thing called Offa's Dyke,*
> *that reacheth farre in length."*
>
> Michael Drayton

The majority of this route is outside Gwent, but it has been included in this guide to provide a full picture of the walking possibilities in this area. Also, many walkers may be interested in following Offa's Dyke Path from Sedbury to Monmouth and returning the next day along the Wye Valley Walk.

Offa's Dyke Path is unique among the other designated long distance routes in Britain in the fact that it follows an archaeological feature rather than a coastline or a range of hills. To walk the total distance of the Path from Sedbury to Prestatyn in North Wales (168 miles), it is advisable to allow about three weeks for the journey. This will provide a reasonable time to look around some of the interesting places on the route. Of course many people prefer to tackle the route in sections or as single day walks.

Several guide books are available that describe the route in considerable detail. Strip maps of the route and general information on accommodation is available from The Offa's Dyke Association, Old Primary School, West Street, Knighton, Powys, LD7 1EW.

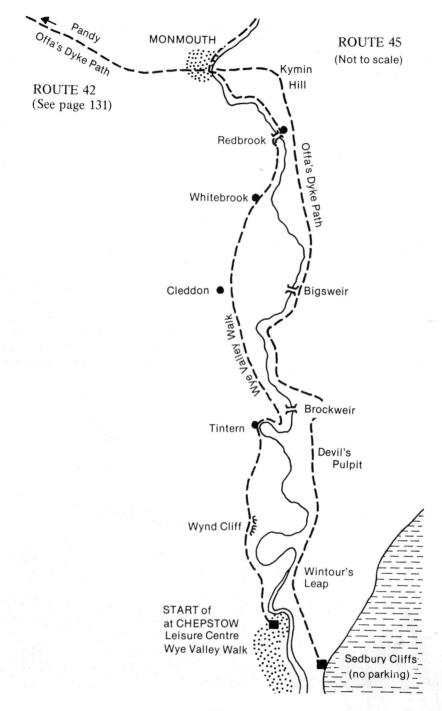

Pandy

Offa's Dyke Path

MONMOUTH

ROUTE 45
(Not to scale)

Kymin
Hill

ROUTE 42
(See page 131)

Offa's Dyke Path

Redbrook

Whitebrook

Cleddon

Bigsweir

Wye Valley Walk

Brockweir

Tintern

Devil's
Pulpit

Wynd Cliff

Wintour's
Leap

START of
at CHEPSTOW
Leisure Centre
Wye Valley Walk

Sedbury Cliffs
(no parking)

Offa was the King of the ancient Kingdom of Mercia and between the period 757 and 795 A.D. he dominated the whole of Britain. He ordered the dyke to be constructed to mark the boundary with Wales and the sections that remain provide a fascinating relic of that period of history. The boundary between England and Wales in present times only follows the dyke in a few places, but they are never far apart.

The southern end of the Dyke is on the Sedbury Cliffs overlooking the Severn, where a large boulder of Conglomerate Sandstone marks the start of this Long Distance Path. It is very adequately waymarked all the way to Monmouth, so it is unnecessary to give a detailed description in this guide, but the following information should prove of interest.

Leaving Sedbury Cliffs, you soon pass through Tutshill and the remains of a stone tower which has been described variously as a watch tower, a 16th century beacon and a ruined windmill. It is also said that Cromwell bombarded Chepstow Castle from here during the Civil War.

A cliff top path is followed to reach the impressive viewpoint of Wintour's Leap. According to local legend, this was the scene of a remarkable horseback escape by Sir John Wintour, who was being chased by Cromwell's Roundheads. He leapt from this point into the river to avoid capture and apparently swam away to safety. Today, this seems an impossible feat, but one must bear in mind that the cliffs have been drastically changed by quarrying since that time. Wintour's Leap is a good viewpoint and the 200 ft limestone cliffs are now very popular with helmeted rock climbers (present day Roundheads!) and the woods below are now protected as a Nature Reserve.

Chepstow Castle   *19th century engraving*

Tintern Abbey from the Devil's Pulpit   *19th century engraving*

The route continues high above the river and other good viewpoints are reached at Shorncliff and the curiously named Devil's Pulpit. This natural platform of rock affords a magnificent view of the valley and from this point the Devil is supposed to have preached to the monks working in Tintern Abbey grounds far below, hoping to entice them from their work.

From here, the Path continues along impressive stretches of the Dyke still intact before it descends at Madgett Hill. Now there is a choice of route and the more pleasant alternative (although it does not follow the line of the Dyke) follows a track to Brockweir and then along the riverside path to Bigsweir Bridge.

After a short section of road walking, the Dyke is rejoined with several sections clearly visible. But on reaching Redbrook, the Dyke is not seen again until just north of Kington in the county of Hereford and Worcester.

The next point of interest after Redbrook and its industrial past is the Naval Temple on Kymin Hill which is owned by the National Trust. At an altitude of 800 ft there is a very fine view of Monmouth and the countryside to the north, providing one of the best panoramas in Gwent. The history of the Temple is described in Route 38.

A footpath leads down via a flight of steps and along the side of May Hill to join the main road leading into Monmouth.

From Monmouth, the route continues through Gwent via Llanvihangel Ystern Llewern, Llantilio Crossenny, White Castle and Llangattock Lingoed to reach the Hatterrall Hill of the Black Mountains. This route is waymarked and provides a fascinating journey for the energetic walker.

General Information

MUSEUMS

Newport Museum, John Frost Square, Newport.
Open: Monday to Saturday 10.00 am — 5.30 pm.

Chepstow Museum, Bridge Street, Chepstow.
Open: May — September, Monday to Saturday 2.00 pm — 5.00 pm.

Rural Crafts Museum, Usk.
Open: Sundays 3.00 pm — 6.00 pm.

Abergavenny & District Museum, Castle Grounds.
Open: Monday to Saturday 11 am — 1 pm & 2 pm — 5 pm.
Sunday 2.30 pm — 5 pm.

Nelson Museum, Priory Street, Monmouth.
Open: Monday to Saturday 10.30 am — 1 pm & 2.15 pm — 6 pm. (April,
May, June, September and October).
Monday to Saturday 10 am — 6 pm, Sunday 2.30 pm — 5.30 pm
(July and August).

Roman Legionary Museum, High Street, Caerleon, near Newport.
Open: Monday to Saturday 11 am — 5 pm, Sunday 2 pm — 5 pm
April to September.

Valley Inheritance Museum, Park Buildings, Pontypool.
Open: All year Monday to Saturday 10 am — 5 pm.
Sunday 2 pm — 5 pm.

Big Pit Mining Museum, Blaenafon.
Open: Daily, May to September, Monday to Saturday 10 am — 5 pm.
Sunday 2 pm — 5 pm.

Blaenafon Ironworks — access limited at present time, as restoration work
is still being undertaken.

Fourteen Locks Canal Interpretation Centre, near Newport.
Open: April to September, 10.30 am — 5 pm.

Tintern Railway Station Exhibition and Picnic Site.
Open: April to December, 10.30 am — 5 pm.

★ ★ ★

WALK LEAFLETS

Leaflets on other walks are available from the reception desk at Gwent
County Council, County Hall, Cwmbrân, and at the Information Centres
listed overleaf.

INFORMATION CENTRES

ABERGAVENNY — Wales Tourist Board and Brecon Beacons National Park Information Centre, 2 Lower Monk Street. Tel. (0873) 3254.

CWMBRÂN — Torfaen District Council, 42 Gwent Square, Cwmbrân, Gwent. Tel. (06333) 67411.

MONMOUTH — National Trust Shop and Wales Tourist Board Information Centre, Church Street, Monmouth. Tel. Monmouth 3270

TINTERN — Wales Tourist Board Information Centre, Abbey Car Park, Tintern. Tel. (02918) 431.

USK — Tourist Information Centre, Old Smithy Gallery, Maryport Street. Tel. (02913) 2207.

CARAVAN AND CAMPING SITES

Up to date and detailed lists are available from the Wales Tourist Board or Tourist Information Centres.

ACCOMMODATION

A list of hotel, inn, motel, guesthouse and farmhouse accommodation is also available from the Wales Tourist Board or Information Centres.

RECOMMENDED READING

Exploring the Brecon Beacons National Park, Barber, C.
Mysterious Wales, Barber, C.
West of the Wye, Barber, W.T.
Exploring Wales, Barber, W.T.
History of Monmouthshire (12 volumes), Bradney, Sir Joseph
Story of Monmouthshire, Clark, A.
Rape of the Fair Country, Cordell, A.
Historical Tour of Monmouthshire, Coxe, W.
Monmouthshire, its History and Topography, Evans, C.J.O.
Here and There in Monmouthshire, Hando, Fred J.
Journeys in Gwent, Hando, Fred J.
The Pleasant Land of Gwent, Hando, Fred J.
Monmouthshire Sketch Book, Hando, Fred J.
Monmouth Town Sketchbook, Hando, Fred J.
Out and About in Monmouthshire, Hando, Fred J.
Monmouthshire, Phillips, O.
Between Mountain and Marsh, Pickford, J.A.F.
Where Wye and Severn Flow, Smart, W.J.
About Chepstow, Waters, I.
The Unfortunate Valentine Morris, Waters, I.

And Finally...
25 Interesting Claims for Gwent

1. There are few areas in Britain where so much variety of landscape, history and culture can be found in such a small area.

2. Gwent has more ruined castles per square mile than any other county in Britain. Twenty five Norman castles were sited in this area.

3. At Caerleon can be seen the best example of a Roman amphitheatre in Britain. It was big enough to seat the entire Roman garrison of 6,000 men.

4. The oldest public house in Wales is the Skirrid Mountain Inn at Llanvihangel Crucorney, near Abergavenny. It is said that this ancient hostelry dates back to the 11th century.

5. The best example of an 18th century ironworks in Britain can be seen at Blaenavon. It is currently being restored by the Department of the Environment and will be open to the public in due course.

6. The longest flight of canal locks in Wales can be seen at Fourteen Locks, near Newport. This intricate system of lock chambers allowed the barges to rise a total height of 168 feet in a distance of half a mile.

7. The highest town in Wales is Brynmawr, situated at an altitude of between 1,250—1,500 feet above sea level.

8. Possibly the second longest flight of steps in Wales are the 365 Steps ascending the Wyndcliff in the Wye Valley (the longest flight being the Roman steps in the Rhinog mountains of North Wales, which are 2,000 in number).

9. The only Transporter Bridge in Britain that is still in working order can be seen at Newport.

10. Also at Newport is the third highest tidal rise in the world, for the Usk on a high tide may rise a height of thirty feet.

11. To see the most crooked church in Britain go to Cwmyoy in the Black Mountains.

12. The highest Country Park in Wales is Pen-y-fan Pond, near Oakdale, situated at an altitude of 1,000 feet.

13. The longest railway tunnel in Britain runs beneath the Severn and connects Gwent with Avon. It is 4½ miles long and was opened in 1886.

14. The largest piece of Conglomerate rock in Wales is the Suck Stone, near Staunton, and it weighs an estimated 14,000 tons.

15. At Monmouth Museum can be seen the largest collection of Nelson relics in the world, which were collected originally by Lady Llangattock, the mother of Charles Rolls.

16. Cwmbrân was the first new town to be built in Wales.

17. West Mon Golf Course at Nantyglo is the highest in Wales with the 13th hole at 1,500 feet above sea level and known as the "Crow's Nest". Thermal underwear is advisable for all who play here!

18. Tintern Abbey has been quoted as "the most beautiful ecclesiastical ruin in Europe".

19. The most famous show jumping horse in the world is buried in Gwent. The grave of Foxhunter may be seen on the Blorenge Mountain.

20. Crumlin Viaduct, now dismantled, was once the longest railway bridge in the world. It was half a mile long and 200 feet high.

21. Raglan Castle was once the home of the wealthiest man in Britain in the 17th century, when the Marquis of Worcester lived there. It also contained the largest collection of Welsh manuscripts in Europe, but this was unfortunately destroyed during the Civil War.

22. Before it was cut down in the late 19th century, the Golynos Oak, near High Cross, was the largest oak tree in Britain.

23. The Severn Estuary is rated as the second most important area in Britain for observing wading birds.

24. At Pontypool Park is the second longest artificial ski slope in Britain.

25. Pontypool Golf Course is the second highest in England and Wales with the 11th hole at an altitude of 1,400 feet.

★ ★ ★ ★ ★

"Departing guest, leave a blessing
On thy footsteps, and may'st thou be blessed:
Health and prosperity be with thee on thy journey
And happiness on thy return."

Translation of a Welsh inscription
on the gatehouse to Llanover estate